# ALICE AND
# OTHER FRIENDS

# BOOKS BY VERNON COLEMAN

The Medicine Men (1975)
 Paper Doctors (1976)
Everything You Want To Know About Ageing (1976)
Stress Control (1978)
The Home Pharmacy (1980)
Aspirin or Ambulance (1980)
Face Values (1981) Guilt (1982)
The Good Medicine Guide (1982)
Stress And Your Stomach (1983)
Bodypower (1983)
An A to Z Of Women's Problems (1984)
Bodysense (1984)
Taking Care Of Your Skin (1984)
Life Without Tranquillisers (1985)
High Blood Pressure (1985)
Diabetes (1985)
Arthritis (1985)
Eczema and Dermatitis (1985)
The Story Of Medicine (1985)
Natural Pain Control (1986)
Mindpower (1986)
Addicts and Addictions (1986)
Dr Vernon Coleman's Guide To Alternative Medicine (1988)
Stress Management Techniques (1988)
Overcoming Stress (1988)
Know Yourself (1988)
The Health Scandal (1988)
The 20 Minute Health Check (1989)
Sex For Everyone (1989)
Mind Over Body (1989)
Eat Green Lose Weight (1990)
Toxic Stress (1991)
Why Animal Experiments Must Stop (1991)
The Drugs Myth (1992)
Why Doctors Do More Harm Than Good (1993)
Stress and Relaxation (1993)
Complete Guide to Sex (1993)

How to Conquer Backache (1993)
How to Conquer Arthritis (1993)
Betrayal of Trust (1994)
Know Your Drugs (1994)
Food for Thought (1994)
The Traditional Home Doctor (1994)
I Hope Your Penis Shrivels Up (1994)
People Watching (1995)
Relief from IBS (1995)
The Parent's Handbook (1995)
Oral Sex: Bad Taste And Hard To Swallow (1995)
Why Is Pubic Hair Curly? (1995)
Men in Dresses (1996)
Power over Cancer (1996)
Crossdressing (1996)
How To Get The Best Out Of Prescription Drugs (1996)
How To Get The Best Out Of Alternative Medicine (1996)
How to Stop Your Doctor Killing You (1996)


novels
The Village Cricket Tour (1990)
The Bilbury Chronicles (1992)
Bilbury Grange (1993)
Mrs Caldicot's Cabbage War (1993)
The Man Who Inherited a Golf Course (1993)
Bilbury Revels (1994)
Deadline (1994)
Bilbury Country (1996)


short stories
Bilbury Pie (1995)


on cricket
Thomas Winsden's Cricketing Almanack (1983)

Diary Of A Cricket Lover (1984)


as Edward Vernon
Practice Makes Perfect (1977)
Practise What You Preach (1978)
Getting Into Practice (1979)
Aphrodisiacs - An Owners Manual (1983)
Aphrodisiacs - An Owners Manual (Turbo Edition) (1984)
The Complete Guide To Life (1984)

as Marc Charbonnier
Tunnel (novel 1980)

with Dr Alan C Turin
No More Headaches (1981)

with Alice
Alice's Diary (1989)
Alice's Adventures (1992)

# ALICE AND
# OTHER FRIENDS

Vernon Coleman

Illustrated by the author

Chilton Designs Publishers

First published in 1996 by Chilton Designs Publishers, Publishing House, Trinity Place, Barnstaple, Devon EX32 9HJ, England.

ISBN: 1 898146 30 6

A catalogue record for this book is available from the British Library.

Printed and bound by:  J W Arrowsmith, Bristol

## Introduction

I love animals. They make wonderful friends. I would like you to meet some of the animals with whom I have been (and in some cases still am) lucky enough to share my life.


Vernon Coleman
1996

'*I once had a sparrow alight upon my shoulder for a moment while I was hoeing in a village garden, and I felt that I was more distinguished by that circumstance than I should have been by any epaulette I could have worn.*'
    Henry David Thoreau

Dedication

In memory of Alice
1983 - 1992

# Timmy, Dick and Harry

I have lived with seven cats and have had close and loving relationships with them all. They have all been very special to me - and even though not all of them are still in this world they are all still as special to me as they ever were.

I shared my boyhood with a cat called Timmy. He had long, grey hair and used to follow me when I went on walks to the local park. I loved him dearly and I carved his name on my school desk.

*"Timmy used to follow me when I went for walks in the park."*

13

Once, when we were on holiday in Switzerland visiting the family of a boy we had met in England, my father used his halting German to explain that we had a cat with long, grey hair. I remember that in response to this carefully enunciated statement the man of the family went to a drawer in a huge sideboard and pulled out a candle. He then showed the candle to each one of us in turn and, with the aid of a complicated mime, showed us that it was entirely bald. We did not wish to appear impolite and so we responded to this apparently bizarre behaviour as politely as we could. We all nodded and marvelled at this hairless candle.

It was only later that we discovered that the words 'cat' and 'candle' are rather similar in German. Our Swiss hosts had clearly thought that my father had said that we had a candle with long, grey hair. They must have been just as puzzled as we were.

* * * *

Timmy died when I was at medical school and was buried on the very edge of a wood which lay adjacent to the garden of my parents' home in Berkshire - in a spot where he regularly used to lie and bask in the sun.

The next two cats with whom I lived were jet black twin brothers called Dick and Harry. I was a general practitioner when they came to live with us and they were both tiny kittens. I remember that once, when he was a young cat, Harry came into the house to fetch me from my typewriter. I thought he just wanted to play but he miaowed and miaowed and wouldn't stop. Eventually I stood up and followed him outside. He took me straight to a tree where Dick had got stuck high above the ground. I rescued Dick with the aid of a step ladder and Dick and I developed a very special friendship. He would sit on my shoulders for hours at a time. He used to love playing games. His favourite game involved my throwing a small clay marble up the stairs while he sat at the top and tried to catch it or stop it before it bounced back down to the bottom. He loved this game and would frequently bring the marble to me while I was working, dropping it at my feet and looking up at me, waiting. If I was out of the house he would drop the marble in one of my

14

slippers so that I would find it the moment I came back into the house.

*"Dick would drop a marble in my slipper and wait for me to come home."*

Dick was run over by a car and buried at the bottom of the garden. I cried for days and was utterly inconsolable. Dick had been a real friend. Dick and Harry had been very close and Harry was distraught too. He wouldn't eat for quite a while, but just kept moping around looking for Dick.

Shortly afterward Dick died we brought Alice and Thomasina home from a cat sanctuary. They were both very tiny and very young and had both been abandoned by their mothers. Alice spent the rest of her life with me. As I write this both Thomasina and I are still alive and, given our advanced years, as well as can be reasonably expected.

Thomasina was originally called Tom because the vet thought she was a he. We changed her name when the error was discovered. Harry taught both Alice and Thomasina to hunt. He would take them out into the garden and make them do as he did but neither Alice nor Thomasina were very keen on their lessons. Harry would crawl ahead, showing them how to stalk, and Alice and Thomasina would crawl behind for a yard or so and then get bored and start to play. Harry would turn round, go back and hit them both around the head sharply enough to bowl them over and for a few moments afterwards they would pay attention. But soon they would be distracted again and the whole ritual would be repeated.

Harry, like Dick, was killed in a road accident. We rushed him to the vet but he was dead when we got him there.

Shortly afterwards I moved to the country. Since then I have never bought a house near to a road and have always chosen properties so remote from road traffic that the risk of a cat being run over is also remote.

## Alice goes paddling

Once I was in a field clearing a stream which had become blocked with twigs and leaves. I was wearing Wellington boots and after a while I waded to the far side of the stream to trim some overhanging, dead branches. Alice, who had been sitting on a fence post, suddenly saw me and came bounding down the field towards me. When she saw that I was on the 'wrong' side of the stream she didn't hesitate. She found the shallowest part and waded across the stream to be with me. Thomasina, who had followed Alice down the field, cried plaintively until I picked her up and carried her across the stream. But Alice just waded through water that came up to her chest.

## Indoor sport for bad weather

On fine, sunny days Alice and Thomasina both used to bring mice into the house and let them go. They would then go outside and start hunting again. It was some time before I realised that they were bringing the mice into the house so that they would have indoor sport to keep them amused when the weather was bad.

(Thomasina is now a little older and slower than she used to be. She does not catch quite so much wildlife and so what she catches she tends to eat).

## Professional courtesy

If Alice found a mouse in the house which had been brought in by Thomasina she would not catch it, kill it or eat it. Somehow she would know that the mouse belonged to Thomasina. The same thing happened the other way around. Thomasina would not catch a mouse which had been originally brought into the house by Alice. I always found it odd to watch Alice staring at a mouse, but showing no professional interest in it.

## An impressive trick

Alice loved to drape herself around my neck. She would stay there for hours - often with her front legs hanging loosely on one side of my neck and her rear legs hanging loosely on the other side of my neck. She was very relaxed about it. She would stay draped around my neck while I played snooker, table tennis or croquet. And she could stay there while I changed my shirt and jumper too. I'm still not quite sure how she would do it but I would take off one jumper and shirt and she would stay exactly where she was. I would then put on a clean shirt and jumper and when I had finished she would still be lying around my neck. It was an impressive trick.

*"Alice used to drape herself around my neck"*

## Making a point

When Tom and Alice didn't like the food we gave them they would always go outside and catch something more to their liking. They would then bring their catch inside and show it to us before they ate it.

## Alice behind the wheel

Alice liked travelling in the car as long as she didn't have to sit in a box or a basket. I remember, in particular, one long journey in a Volvo estate car which I used to own. Alice and Thomasina spent part of the journey standing up at the back of the car with their paws resting on the bottom of the rear window, watching the cars behind. Alice then discovered that she could crawl underneath my seat. She thought that

*"Alice liked driving in the car"*

was a wonderful hiding place. Then she tried lying on the dashboard. When she was there I couldn't see much of the road ahead because she blocked a large chunk of the windscreen so I gently persuaded her to move. She ended up with her hind legs on the seat between my thighs and her front legs resting on the steering wheel. She completed the journey like that; looking for all the world as though she was helping me to drive.

## Alice on TV

Alice used to love sitting on top of the television set. I think she liked the television set because it was warm. She used to leap on top of the

*"Alice used to love to sit on top of the TV set"*

set and knock anything else that happened to be there flying onto the floor. A good many plant pots were broken that way. From time to time hairs had to be cleaned out of the back of the television set. Alice used to like to sit with her tail hanging down across the screen. Occasionally, she would swish it from side to side for no apparent reason. We used to have to record programmes we wanted to watch so that we could view them at a time when she was happily sleeping somewhere else. The only programme she really liked was snooker. She used to try to catch the balls as they moved around on the table. Her favourite snooker player was former world champion Alex 'Hurricane' Higgins. He was a favourite of hers because he made the balls move around very quickly.

## An unavoidable fact of nature

I heard a hunter claim that the fox is a just target for the barbaric social activity of hunting on the inaccurate grounds that it too kills for pleasure. I do not believe that it is true that a fox will kill chickens or geese for pleasure. Killing for pleasure is a purely human emotion. It is something which we can understand. And so we wrongly attach this exclusively human label to another animal. Foxes kill to survive. They will kill anything which they, or their dependants, can eat and they will kill anything which might inconveniently draw attention to their presence. (It is for this reason that they often kill all the hens in a chicken run but take only a few). We might not like the fact that foxes kill. And it might be commercially inconvenient. But it is an unavoidable fact of nature. When he has finished killing the fox will carry away as much food as he can carry. (If he has killed more than he can carry at one time he will make several trips if it is safe to do so.)

# Thomasina gets lost

Thomasina got lost one day. We looked everywhere for her. Eventually, after hunting for her for several hours we heard a very faint miaow coming from deep in the middle of an extensive patch of nettles and brambles growing alongside a small stagnant pond. I remember that it was late in the afternoon but it was a hot day and the stench from the pond was awful. With the aid of a variety of garden tools (including a machete, a scythe and various other cutting instruments) we chopped, slashed, cut and hacked our way through the undergrowth towards the source of the miaowing. We were utterly convinced that Thomasina was trapped and lost. Every few moments we called to her and every few moments we heard her faint reply.

After four or five hours solid labour we found her, just as it was getting dark. We were soaked with sweat and bleeding from bramble scratches. The bits of skin which weren't bleeding were swollen from nettle stings. Thomasina was crouched next to the foul smelling stagnant pond and when we had cut away the brambles and nettles which remained in front of her she put her head slightly on one side and gazed at us rather quizzically, as though to say: 'Hello! How nice to see you! What are you doing here?' But she didn't move. Her fur had collected all sorts of bits of debris and her paws were muddy and wet.

I bent down, stroked her head and picked her up.

Nestled in my arms Thomasina rubbed her head against me, to let me know that she was pleased to see me, and then miaowed rather more loudly. Then she wriggled a little to let me know that she wanted to get back down to the ground. I opened my arms and stooped down so that she didn't have too far to jump. As soon as she landed she walked carefully back to where she had been sitting when we had reached her. She looked at me, turned round and settled down again quite happily.

She hadn't been lost at all.

We picked up our tools and walked wearily back to the house.

# Alice and the can of cream

We used to keep an aerosol can of cream in the kitchen - the sort of can where, when you press the top, synthetic, creamy, foam comes out, suitable for putting onto fruit and other puddings. Alice acquired a taste for this cream. She found out how to get the cream out of the can by pressing the button on the top of the can. She used to lick up the cream she squirted out of the can so that it was impossible to see what she had been doing. For a while I was under the impression that the cream company wasn't filling the cans properly. And then I caught her at it. As always, when she was caught doing something which she knew she wasn't supposed to be doing Alice would suddenly start to wash herself.

*"Alice found out how to get the cream out of the can by pressing the button on the top."*

## Bad manners

The first time I found a mouse hiding in the house I spent ages trying to catch it in a shoe box. Alice and Thomasina both sat nearby watching. They made absolutely no attempt to take part in the 'hunt' for they clearly felt that this would have been bad manners. When one of them has initiated a hunt in the house the other will watch but never, ever interfere.

## Two birds and the sea

A tanker had sunk off the Welsh coast and its vast cargo had been pouring into the sea for hours. I walked for several miles along the clifftops of North Devon and was filled with a deep, dark despair for the sea, covered with a thin layer of oil, had turned a peculiarly unpleasant shade of brown. Normally, the sea along this stretch of coastline is more white than blue for the wind constantly whips the waves into surf and foam. The sea crashes onto the rocks noisily and furiously. But on this day, although there was plenty of wind, there was no foam. Instead, the sea lapped on the rocks silently and stickily. The oil lay on the surface of the sea like a huge brown blanket. As I watched from high above on the clifftop path there was a small flash of activity a couple of hundred yards out to sea. I stared with horror as an oil covered cormorant struggled in vain to escape from the sea. Three or four times the bird fought to break free from the film of oil. Each time it failed. And then, as it sank below the surface, it disappeared from view. I watched as another cormorant flew low over the sea, looking for somewhere to set down. I willed him not to settle in this contaminated sea but to fly on; to fly away to some safer stretch of coastline; to try and find some patch of relatively unpolluted sea. Eventually, this second cormorant disappeared from sight - still flying and still searching for a safe, blue stretch of sea.

What I had seen on that dismal day was yet another example of man's callous regard for nature. And yet another example of the earth's wildlife paying the price.

## Alice and Thomasina at school

When Alice and Thomasina were very small they occasionally annoyed Harry. Harry did not have much of a paternal instinct. One day the three of them were in the garden. Harry had been trying to teach Alice and Thomasina how to hunt. As usual they had not been paying much attention. They wanted to play not learn.

*"Harry was quite cross when he turned round and saw that Alice and Thomasina were not paying attention."*

Suddenly, Harry hit poor Thomasina such a blow that she rolled over on the grass several times (she wasn't at all hurt and seemed only surprised). Harry then leapt eight feet into the air onto a flat roof on a small outbuilding. He stayed there, sunning himself for the rest of the afternoon and put off his arduous teaching duties until another day.

## Thomasina writes

Thomasina walked across my computer keyboard one morning. In order to print something which appears on the screen it is necessary to press two keys simultaneously. The keys are about 20 cm apart on the keyboard. Somehow Thomasina succeeded in pressing them both and her work was duly printed.

Here is what she wrote.

99999999999999999000000000000000877777yhojsadgtAxcv
rmuhbtttttttttttttttttttttttttttttttttttttttttttttttttttttttttttttttg
vrdeeeeeeeeeeeeeeeeeeeeeeeeeeeeeeeeee3222222222222222qa2AAAAAAAA
A A A A A A A A A A A A A 2 2 2 2 2 2 2 2 2 2 2 2 2 2 2 2
IUUUUUUUUUUUUUUUUUU.

Maybe Thomasina should apply for a government grant to continue her work. But there again she is probably too intelligent to receive a government grant.

## Not fair!

Alice had a bad foot one day. The vet told us that we had to keep her in. She was very unhappy about staying in. She kept looking at me as if to say: 'It's not fair. I've got a bad foot AND I'm being kept in.'

*"Alice kept looking at me as if to say 'Its not fair! I've got a bad foot AND I'm being kept in!'"*

# Bottle fed lambs

The four sheep who live with me were bottle fed as lambs. They were a lot of trouble when they were young. (They are still a lot of trouble). The two twins - Cilla and Karen - both had severe diarrhoea and nearly died. Snowy had the same problem and she too was seriously ill. Septimus seemed to be the healthiest of the four and she certainly had healthy bowels but even she worried us. She had a funny turn one day when she got over excited running around and around the house. We took her to the veterinary hospital in the back of the estate car. They could find absolutely nothing wrong with her. Miraculously and mysteriously Septimus got better as quickly as she had fallen ill. The vet discharged her and said he didn't have the faintest idea what had been wrong with her. She insisted on standing up in the car on the way home. We had put a piece of plastic down in case of accidents but the car was never quite the same again.

# Sheep are not stupid

Someone who lives in a town said to me that he was surprised I kept sheep because they are such stupid animals. I suspect that this myth has been sustained by those who have a financial interest in our eating bits of meat carved from dead sheep and lambs. It is much easier to persuade us to accept the idea of sheep standing around in the rain and the wind, without shelter, or being crammed into dark, overcrowded sheds and then being chopped into bits, if we think of the animals as being stupid. More human beings would feel uncomfortable if they felt they were eating someone as intelligent as themselves.

Despite the myth about the stupidity of sheep if you talk to farmers who look after sheep they will acknowledge that sheep are truly extremely intelligent animals. They are stubborn and they are extremely nervous creatures but neither of these qualities are by any means the same as stupidity. I know lots of stubborn and nervous people who would be outraged if it was assumed that they were automatically also stupid.

## Favourite places

Here is a list of Alice's ten favourite sleeping places:
1. Wrapped around my neck.
2. On the top shelf in the airing cupboard.
3. In her basket on top of the central heating boiler.
4. In another basket on top of an eight foot tall bookcase in my study.
5. On a pile of spare blankets stored underneath our bed.
6. On top of a pile of old cushions stored in the former chicken house.
7. On the bonnet of the car when put into the garage after a long drive.
8. On a pile of logs stored in the shed where the ride-on mower lived.
9. Underneath a fir tree overlooking the driveway.
10. On my desk, next to my typewriter.

## Alice was not a pet

I have never liked the concept of cat 'ownership'. I have never owned a cat in my life - though I have shared my life with quite a number, and they have certainly played a most important part in my life. Alice and I, for example, had an equal relationship. We were certainly not 'master' and 'pet'.

## Introducing the sheep

The two black faced sheep - Karen and Cilla - are twins. When they were very small they were completely black. We called them Karen and Cilla after Karen Black (the actress) and Cilla Black (the singer and TV celebrity). Snowy got her name because she was so white and clean. And Septimus had the number seven painted on her side.

All four sheep love being shown physical affection - they very much enjoy having their necks and heads stroked and they adore being given a back massage. If Karen doesn't get all the cuddling and stroking and tickling and massaging she wants she kicks out and gives a fairly firm reminder with her left front leg.

## Alice and Trigger

At one time we had a horse called Trigger staying with us for a while. When the weather was sunny we fed Trigger outside, using a black feeding box which hooked over the top bar of the wooden fence surrounding the field. One morning I went out to fill the feeding box and had quite a surprise when Alice suddenly popped her head out of the box. I had never seen a cat-in-the box before. She looked at me and looked at Trigger, who was standing nearby. The horse looked at Alice, walked gently forwards and slowly lowered his head to within an inch or two of Alice. Alice, quite unafraid, lifted her head. The two noses, one huge and one small, touched briefly. It was a wonderful moment. Naturally, I did not have a camera with me.

## Alice's fan club

At Christmas time Alice always used to receive a good many cards and presents from readers of her two books. She had - and still has - a large and enthusiastic fan club. Many of the cards were signed with the names of other cats - and these were often accompanied by photographs. There were several tom cats who were, I was told, very 'keen' on Alice. I'm not at all sure what she would have made of that. Quite a few readers used to remember Thomasina too.

*"At Christmas Alice always used to receive lots of cards and presents.
Happily Thomasina used to receive lots too!"*

## Karen surprises the vet

I tried to teach the four sheep who share my life their own names -
with some considerable success. By using each sheep's name when I
talked to her I got each one to recognise the sound as meaning something special to her. I called Karen to me in the shippen one day while
the vet was there - not simply to demonstrate how 'clever' she was
but simply because the vet needed to look at her foot. As Karen walked
gingerly over towards us the vet told me that he had never seen a
sheep respond to its name before. I think he was rather surprised.

*"The vet told me he had never before seen a sheep respond to its name"*

## Septimus and the deckchair

When Septimus was very small she used to love to follow me around
and do whatever I was doing. If I was sitting on the swing seat she had
to sit on the swing seat alongside me. If I was sitting in a deckchair
then she had to have a deckchair too. One day, when I didn't get up
and fetch her a deckchair of her own quickly enough, she leapt up
onto my lap when I was sitting in a deck chair. The canvas split and
the deckchair collapsed depositing us both on the floor.

## Flock Master

Anyone who has custodial care of four or more sheep is officially
known as a 'flock master'. I was going to change my occupation on
my passport to 'flock master' but when I renewed my passport I discovered that the authorities no longer wanted me to list any occupation at all. I do, however, sometimes put 'flock master' down on official forms. A more inappropriate term it is difficult to imagine.

## Alice on the roof

Alice hated having workmen around the house. I don't know whether
this was a disaffection she acquired from me or whether it was just a
natural feeling which we shared. At one point we lived in a large, old
house and since I am incapable of doing anything practical or handy
there were often workmen around. Whenever there were painters,
decorators, builders, plumbers, carpenters, electricians or tradesmen
of any other variety around the house Alice would disappear until they
had gone. She would reappear (as if by magic) within moments of
their disappearance.

At one time we had a man working on and around the house for
several months. Alice never got used to his presence and always used
to hide when he arrived. He was a pleasant enough fellow but how-

31

ever much he tried he never really managed to persuade Alice to trust him. This was not his fault at all for Alice was a cautious cat and there were very, very few people whom she felt she knew well enough to trust.

As far as Alice was concerned the thing she liked least about the workman was his habit of walking around the house whistling. He had a peculiar talent for being able to whistle slightly off key and slightly out of tune.

I knew her favourite hiding places and could usually find her without too much difficulty. If she was inside the house she would usually either be in the airing cupboard, on top of one of the bookcases in my study, underneath the bed or, if the door to it had been left open, in the cellar. Outdoors there were several sheds that she liked and I always made sure that doors or windows to these were left open so that she could get in and out easily enough.

She liked the shed where we kept the large, ride on mower and she liked an old chicken shed where there were all sorts of spiders and mice to hunt and where we kept the cushions for the swing seat and, after she had discovered that she could wriggle under the door, she liked the tack room which was built onto the side of the stable. There were, naturally enough, also several bushes and trees which she frequently favoured with her presence.

But on one sunny day I just couldn't find her anywhere. I didn't have the faintest idea where she had hidden herself.

And then, as I walked back to the house, having more or less given up the search, I heard a faint miaow.

I looked around but couldn't see Alice and, more to the point, I couldn't see anywhere at all where she could be hiding. There were no sheds, bushes or other suitable hiding places within fifteen or twenty yards of where I was standing.

I heard the miaow for a second time. It was still very faint but there was no mistaking it: it was Alice.

I looked all around me. I looked underneath the oil tank. I looked in the porch. I looked in the outside lavatory. And then I looked up.

Alice was sitting on top of the chimney. Right on the very top of the chimney pot. She had climbed as high as she possibly could.

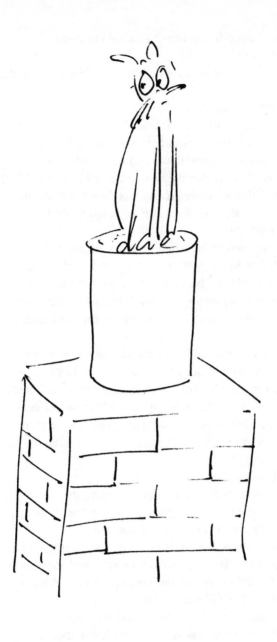

*"Alice was perched right on top of the chimney pot."*

With a lump in my throat I called her name.

Tentatively, Alice slid a paw down the side of the chimney pot as though about to start climbing down. She quickly pulled the paw back.

I called her again.

She repeated the manoeuvre.

This went on for about fifteen minutes. I called her name. She moved as though to come down and then withdrew.

It was obvious that she was frozen with fear and far too frightened to come down by herself. By this time I still had the lump in my throat but I was also getting a stiff neck from bending my head back so that I could watch her.

Hearing me calling Alice's name repeatedly the workman came out of the house to see what was going on. I explained. He looked up. 'I'll fetch the ladders,' he said, very matter of fact and businesslike.

After he had connected the ladders together and put them in position he moved towards the bottom of the ladder, ready to start to climb up.

I have no real head for heights and the roof was a long, long way above the ground but I felt I had to try. 'Let me go!' I said.

A few moments later, breathing heavily, and clinging to the ladder as though my life depended upon it, which, on reflection, I suppose it did, I stood level with the guttering, where the tops of the walls of our house met the bottom edge of the roof, trying hard not to look down.

I called to Alice.

This time, with me so much closer, she made a little more progress. She put two paws down the side of the chimney pot. But she was still too frightened to move all the way.

By now, from the encouragement being offered from below, I realised that I had attracted an enthusiastic and supportive audience. A delivery van driver and his companion and a couple of nearby farmers had arrived to offer helpful encouragement.

After another half an hour I realised that we were getting absolutely nowhere. Alice was stuck. And I knew that if I didn't make a move very quickly I too would be stuck. My fingers were gripping the top of the ladder so tightly that they had gone quite numb. With great reluctance, and considerable care, I clambered back down the ladder. It felt good to have the solid earth under my feet again. I felt I understood just how poor Alice felt.

'I'll go up,' said the workman bravely. 'I'll climb up on the roof.'

And he did too. We didn't have any crawling boards but somehow he managed to pull himself up over the edge of the roof and crawl up to the bottom of the chimney. Once there he pulled himself upright and stood up alongside the chimney. I had never before realised just what tall chimneys we had. Even standing up to his full height he could not reach Alice.

Mind you, even if he had been able to reach Alice I wouldn't have been happy about him trying to do so. I knew very well that if he touched Alice - let alone tried to hold her - she would wriggle and claw and scratch him until he bled and let her go. And I was frightened that he and Alice would come tumbling down off the roof in one great mess of arms, legs, claws, oaths and blood.

'How did she get up there?' asked the delivery driver.

'Easy!' I said, pointing out the route she had taken. 'She climbed onto the oil tank, jumped a couple of feet onto that gently sloping roof there - the one over the back porch - and then from there just walked up onto the main roof.'

'Seems easy enough,' said the delivery driver. 'For a cat,' he added.

'Perhaps we should call the fire brigade?' suggested the farmer.

The nearest fire brigade engine was at least half an hour away. It would, I thought, probably be dark by then. But I was still thinking about what the delivery driver had said. It hadn't been a difficult climb. Indeed, for Alice it must have been a very easy climb. Her problem now was simply that she was frozen with fear. All she needed was a little encouragement.

'Can you meet me at the guttering?' I called up to the workman.

He smiled, nodded and crawled carefully down the roof. I climbed up the ladder. When I got to the top of the ladder I whispered to the workman. 'Would you mind going back up to the top of the roof and whistling?' I asked him.

'You think that might persuade her to come down?'

I said I thought it would.

The workman looked rather pleased. 'Be delighted,' he said. 'Is there anything in particular you'd like me to whistle?'

I said I didn't think it mattered terribly much what he whistled.

I didn't tell him this, of course, but I thought that if Alice was more alarmed by what was going on around her than she was by the prospect of sliding down the chimney pot and walking down the roof then she might make the necessary move.

And that is exactly what happened.

The workman went up onto the roof. He whistled 'When The Saints Go Marching In' and Alice, alarmed and horrified by this development, decided that she disliked the workman's whistling much more than she was frightened of climbing down the chimney pot.

About thirty seconds later she was jumping off the oil tank onto my shoulders none the worse for her adventure. I gave the workman a well earned bonus.

After that I don't think Alice ever even jumped up onto the oil tank any more. And she certainly never set foot on the house roof again.


## The sheep dip

When the sheep were young a local farmer kindly agreed to take them through his sheep dip bath. At the time it was compulsory for all 'flock masters' to have all their sheep dipped every year. Cilla, Karen, Septimus and Snowy went just once.

There was a good deal of mud around the sheep dip and since they didn't like getting their feet wet or muddy all four of them had to be carried over the mud. The farmer thought this was very odd. But then I think he thought we were odd for keeping sheep for no apparent reason.

Naturally enough, none of them liked the sheep dip itself. They came out shaking themselves and looking very miserable. We dried them with towels and blankets and gave them chocolate digestive biscuits as a special treat. I vowed that whatever the rules were there wasn't a government on the globe that would be able to force me to send them through a sheep dip ever again. And that was, indeed, the last time they went through a sheep dip.

## Trigger's new shoes

Trigger, the horse who was staying with us, needed new shoes and so the farrier was called. He arrived with his dog, a small and noisy terrier. While the farrier did his work outside the stable I worked in the garden writing one of my Bilbury novels. We were separated by a

*"Get your sheep off me and my dog"*

very high, very thick yew hedge. Twenty minutes or so after the farrier's arrival the terrier started making even more noise and I heard the farrier shout 'Get away!' A few moments later I heard the farrier cry out: 'Hey! Come and get your sheep off me and my dog!' I stopped work, walked around to the stable and saw the farrier and his dog backed up against the stable wall. Septimus, Snowy, Cilla and Karen, were lined up around them as though holding them prisoner. The terrier was barking away for all he was worth but the sheep were taking absolutely no notice of him. Trigger the horse, now the proud owner of a set of new shoes, was standing nearby watching. 'Get these sheep off me!' cried the farrier when he saw me.

Trying not to laugh out loud I called to the sheep, who had no aggressive intentions whatsoever but merely hoped to be given cuddles or biscuits or possibly even both.

Hearing my voice the four sheep lost all interest in the farrier and turned and walked towards me.

Over the years there must have been thousands of occasions when sheep have been worried by dogs but I suspect that this might have been the first time in history that a dog (not to mention a farrier) has been worried by sheep.

## Lamb chops

'How long do sheep live?' I asked a farmer, out of idle curiosity.

He admitted that he didn't know.

'How long do sheep live?' I asked an expert in these matters.

He scratched his neck and thought for a moment. 'I'm not sure,' he confessed.

The reason for this ignorance is, of course, quite simple.

Very few sheep have a natural life span.

We kill many before they reach adulthood so that we can eat lamb chops.

We kill the rest when they are too old to reproduce.

And we call ourselves civilised.

# The missing swallows

I love swallows. I love the way they play together. I love the way that they return, year after year, to the same barn and the same nest. I love the deep sense of companionship they show towards one another.

I find it enormously impressive that every autumn the swallows leave England and fly to Africa where they spend the winter. And that in the spring they fly all the way back again.

It is a journey of several thousand miles and not all of them make the journey safely. Some are blown off course by the wind and die of hunger and exhaustion. But many die when, as they cross the Mediterranean sea, they make the deadly mistake of landing in Malta to rest and seek food and temporary shelter.

The Maltese must surely be among the cruelest people in the world. They trap and kill birds by the thousand. Some they stuff and sell to collectors. Some they eat. Birds which are unwanted for stuffing or eating are just killed anyway - for fun. One of their favourite tricks for catching birds is to put one bird into a net. When the bird, trapped, cries out in fear and distress other birds come to its aid. The hunters then throw a second net over the new birds - trapping them.

Every autumn, I watch the swallows fly away with sadness in my heart for I know that many will never return. The Maltese will kill some as they fly south for the winter. And they will kill many more as they fly north during the spring.

I want to cry out to the swallows: 'Don't go anywhere near Malta!'

# Going for a walk

At my last house Alice and Thomasina used to regularly go for a walk with me around the boundary of the field (two or three acres in area) in which the four sheep lived.

Sometimes Alice would deliberately lag behind - allowing a

fifty yard gap to separate her from Thomasina and I. She would then run as fast as she could (quite an impressive sight) across the field and leap up onto my shoulders when she was still several feet away from me. I would then have to carry her around the rest of the field on my shoulders. That was her idea of 'going for a walk'.

Thomasina occasionally liked to be carried but she usually just trotted along behind me, sniffing at every interesting smell and doing a little territory marking every now and then.

*"Alice's idea of going for a walk."*

# Having fun

When they were small the lambs used to race round and round the house at breakneck speed. I couldn't keep up with them. Their racing circuit started outside the snooker room window. They would assemble by a wooden bench I used to sit on during summer evenings and would take it in turns to start the race Suddenly, one of them would make a dash for it, trying to get a good head start on the others and one by one four fluffy tails would disappear from view.

Once, after a dozen circuits, they didn't reappear. I waited for a few moments wondering what could have happened to them. Eventually, curiosity got the better of me. I got up from where I was sitting in the garden and started to walk around the house looking for them. I discovered that they had managed to push open the back door and were having great fun in the kitchen. It was then that I discovered that nothing in this world can make quite as much mess in such a short space of time as four lambs having fun.

# Friendship

Friendship is one of the most important assets in anyone's life.

You should take great care of your friends. They are the most valuable asset you have. Choose your friends with care and then treasure them. Your loyalty to true friends should take precedence over everything else in your life.

Remember too, that to win a new friend you must first *be* a friend. And you must work at that friendship. You must invest time and energy and caring. True friendship is an asset which will never tarnish and never devalue. And no one will ever be able to take it away from you.

Oh, and there is one more thing: a friend does not have to be a human being.

## Welcome visitors

Someone I know gets very cross if swallows or house martins choose to make nests around his house. He says they make a lot of mess.

I, on the other hand, am always honoured if birds choose to live with me.

A pair of swallows have decided to build a nest about two feet above my study window. I love watching them fly to and fro with their beakfuls of mud and other nest-building materials.

It is a humbling experience to watch birds build a nest. They work at a pace and with a precision beyond most of today's builders.


## Unwelcome visitors

A pack of hunters went through a wood where I take regular walks. I am appalled to think of the trauma a hunt must do to the animals, birds and other creatures living in that wood - or, indeed, on any other stretch of land. It is not only the animal they choose to chase which suffers. It is difficult to imagine the mayhem, the fear and the damage that a hunt can do in obtaining just a few minutes of 'pleasure'. Badgers, moles, rats, mice, foxes, deer and a thousand other varieties of living being must suffer enormously so that this small and privileged group of vandals can get a quick thrill. Wilde was right when he described the hunt as the 'unspeakable in pursuit of the uneatable'. Why do human beings consider they have the right to treat someone else's territory with such arrogant contempt? How would the hunters feel if a gang of blood thirsty giants drove or galloped through Mayfair, down the Champs Elysées or across Fifth Avenue? It is difficult not to feel an almost constant shame at being a member of the human race.

## Moving house

We were moving house. I didn't want to put Alice or Thomasina into baskets (Alice hated being put into a cage and had quite literally destroyed one 'specially strengthened' 'approved' and 'escape proof' basket with her claws and her teeth) and so I put them both on leads.

*"Alice destroyed an escape proof travelling basket."*

Neither of them minded the leads, which were fitted with body harnesses for comfort and added security. Once, when we had stayed in a flat at the seaside for a few days, they had come for late evening walks around the town while wearing their leads. It was a quiet town and there were few people around at that time of day.

But on this occasion the excitement (and, in particular, the constant coming and going of the removal men) was just too much for

Alice. She panicked, struggled and somehow managed to extricate herself from her body harness. She then managed to get a front leg through her collar as she tried to wriggle out of that as well.

One of the removal men kindly stopped and offered to hold her while I unfastened and then refastened the tiny buckles on the straps of the harness and the collar. Alice relaxed for a moment, lulling us both into a false sense of security. I unfastened the body harness and the collar, released her trapped leg and fastened the collar again.

Alice, who had been waiting for the right moment, decided that she had had enough and was going to make a break for it. She bit, she scratched, she spat, she arched her back and she wriggled. Alice was an unbelievable wriggler. And the removal man, not surprisingly perhaps, let go. As he retreated, pale, shocked and bleeding, to examine his clawed and bitten hands, and I leapt, despairingly and ineffectively after her, Alice raced off along the terrace, down the steps, across the garden, over the fence and into a dense stretch of wild woodland on a steep slope, dragging her lead behind her. Thomasina, who had been sitting quietly on the terrace, watched all this in silent and stunned amazement.

I raced after Alice, along the terrace, down the steps, across the garden, over the fence and into the wood. I saw her, twenty or thirty yards ahead of me along a narrow path through the wood, as she paused and looked behind her to see if anyone was following. I moved gently and slowly and spoke to her. She stared at me and waited, clearly trying to decide what to do. Then there was a shout from behind me as the well intentioned removal man came charging down the garden to 'help'. Alice was off in a flash.

Calling to the removal man to stay where he was I raced blindly along the woodland path, tripping over half hidden roots, crashing into low hanging branches and being scratched by bramble bushes. Occasionally, I caught sight of a flash of black, white and brown as Alice ran quickly and easily through the woodland. I could see her lead still dragging behind her.

Suddenly, I stopped, frightened that by chasing her I was simply pushing Alice further and further away from her own home territory. I called out to her, paused for a moment and then slowly, sadly, retreated; my heart was pounding and there were tears pouring down my cheeks.

I remember little of the rest of that day. The removal men, who had by now finished packing, went away to unload our furniture, books and belongings at the new house while I stayed behind, with Thomasina for company, to await Alice's return.

I sat on the steps, where Alice would be able to see me if and when she finally reappeared from the wood, with tears still pouring down my cheeks, and thought about the terrible things that could happen to her. She might get lost. Her collar might get caught in a tree.

Thomasina sat beside me or on my lap and was a constant and loving source of comfort; she was silent and distressed too. She frequently rubbed her head against me and licked my hand.

I remember that at one point some holiday makers angrily shouted at me to go and move my car which was apparently causing something of an obstruction. I glowered and snarled at them and they went away. I didn't go and move the car. I wasn't going to move from the garden in case Alice came back, didn't see me and ran away again.

I sat there for hour after hour, with my eyes firmly fixed on the fence over which Alice had disappeared. The removal men had left in the morning. Lunchtime came and went. And so did the afternoon. Soon it was dusk. But I did not dare move out of the garden. I wanted to be sure that I would be there whenever Alice returned. I wanted her to see me, and Thomasina, sitting in the garden waiting for her. I knew that she would want to make sure that there was no one else around. But I also suspected that if she did not see me she would not come into the garden at all.

Eventually, as it started to go dark I saw her.

She was sitting on a fence post, ears alert, looking around. The lead was still attached to her. She was covered in bits of leaf and pieces of bramble. She was dishevelled and looked tired. She looked across at me.

'Hello, Alice,' I said, quietly. 'There's no one else here,' I added, reassuringly.

*"Hello, Alice!" I said quietly.*

After pausing there for what seemed a lifetime and a half, looking, watching and thinking, Alice clambered down the fence post and walked towards me. She moved slowly and wearily. I stayed where I was. I didn't want to frighten her. Thomasina, ears pricked, stayed beside me, also waiting.

Moments later the three of us embraced; stroking, hugging, purring, crying, forgiving, welcoming and loving. I removed the collar from around Alice's neck and fetched two saucers and a tin of their favourite cat food from the otherwise empty kitchen.

The two of them ate their fill and then I carried them both to the car and we drove to the new house.

## Alice on my knees

I wrote the two 'Alice' books with Alice sitting on my knees. She enjoyed being with me as I wrote or typed. I always felt that Alice really did 'write' the books and I always thought of them as her books. She even sat on my lap when I did some of the illustrations. I had to throw away many attempts because she had nudged me while I was drawing.

*"I 'wrote' the two 'Alice' books with the author sitting on my knees."*

## Prrrrrrp

Alice had her sad moments (visitors were her most particular hate - she loathed strangers) but I never knew any living creature who enjoyed life so much, or who brought so much happiness into the lives of those around her. Whenever she saw me coming her tail would instantly become vertical, she would run towards me and, with a sound which I can only describe as a 'prrrrrp', leap onto my neck or shoulders.

## Hiding places

Alice used to find the most amazing hiding places. She was for ever discovering ever more unlikely and private spots where she could be warm, private and cosy - and, ideally, able to keep half an eye on the rest of the world so that she need never be surprised. She hated surprises almost as much as she hated visitors.

## Shorn and shivering

Farmers used to shear sheep just once a year. The shearing benefited both parties. The farmers made a little money by selling the wool. And the sheep benefited too - they did not have to wear their thick, woollen coats during the summer months. But many farmers have got greedy. Many now shear their sheep twice a year so that they will have twice as much wool to sell. Without their warm coats the sheep just have to shiver during the colder months. Many die of the cold. But the farmers make enough extra money from the additional wool to cover the cost of the sheep who die. Think of this next time you drive past a field full of sheep - or when you buy a woolly jumper.

# The old chicken house

Alice loved sheds. The older, the mustier, the more cobwebby and the more packed with junk the more she liked them. Her favourite shed was a huge old place that had once been a chicken house. In it we used to store garden furniture, the cushions for the swing seat, flower pots, various bits and pieces of garden equipment that wouldn't fit into the potting shed, all the ladders, a huge roll of black plastic that we had bought to stop the weeds growing, several rolls of wire netting and so on. You can tell how large the shed was by the fact that we also kept the table tennis table in there (set up and quite operational).

I didn't even know Alice could get into this shed until one day when we had visitors and she had run off and I couldn't find her anywhere. I had searched the house, the gardens, the garage, the barn, the stable and all the other sheds and hadn't been able to find her anywhere. In desperation I looked into the old chicken house and found that Alice was in there. She was fast asleep on top of the huge pile of cushions which fitted an old but exceedingly comfortable swing seat which we had bought for £15 at a country house auction a year or two earlier. There were six cushions, each of them six inches thick. Alice was sleeping on about three feet of foam rubber.

Not knowing how on earth she had managed to get into the shed I looked around and discovered that she had managed to slide to one side a tiny wooden door at floor level that had been installed to let the chickens move in and out of the shed.

The door had, I knew, been closed and latched. But Alice, searching for somewhere new to hide, had managed to unlatch it and to slide it open.

Since we didn't have any chickens, and therefore no reason to fear foxes, I left the small door open. From that day on the old chicken house was one of Alice's favourite outdoor hiding places. It was her private domain.

She loved the shed so much that I left the swing seat cushions stacked exactly where they were so that Alice could use them whenever she wanted to. I think that those six cushions probably made the most comfortable cat bed ever discovered anywhere in the entire history of the known universe. I had to buy fresh cushions for the swing seat but it was well worth it to know that Alice had such a good and comfortable hiding place for those rare occasions when we had visitors.

## An obscene and barbaric business

I was with Cilla when Karen, who was sitting on the grass about a hundred yards away, rose to her feet and started to walk towards me. I noticed with horror that she was limping. As I set off across the field to her Cilla watched me carefully. Suddenly she took off and ran across the field to be with her twin sister. She had overtaken me and was standing alongside her sister when I arrived. (I have never been able to run as quickly as the sheep. Although they are overweight they are astonishingly fast and can cover a hundred yards quicker than any man I know.)

While I examined Karen's foot Cilla stood patiently by, as though waiting for the diagnosis. These two animals are so close that I confess it rather frightens me. I know that if anything ever happens to one of them then whichever one remains will be inconsolable.

It saddens me to think that every day of the week thousands of sheep are parted from their sisters, mothers and brothers. What a miserable, obscene, barbaric business the meat business is. Thousands of sensitive creatures like Karen and Cilla are packed into lorries every day. Terrified and overcrowded they are driven for hours and sometimes days before being herded into slaughterhouses where they are cruelly mistreated and finally killed.

It alarms me to realise that if Karen and Cilla had not come to live with me they would both have been dead - and eaten - years ago. The thought of it fills me with despair.

I think that perhaps the only solution is to try to turn the sadness into anger and the anger into literary action.

## Alice and the fox

I once watched Alice and a fox sniffing one another. Alice was clearly not quite sure what to make of the fox and the fox was equally clearly not at all sure what to do about Alice. Eventually, they backed away from one another and called it a draw.

## "Now look what you've made me do!"

If I was busy working and I delayed giving Alice a meal she would come and look at me with a look that clearly said: 'If you don't feed me now I will go out, catch a mouse and bring it in.' And, if for some reason I failed to respond, she would then go out, catch a mouse and drop it at my feet. She would look up at me as if to say: 'Now, look what you've made me do!' And she would then proceed to eat the mouse, making a great deal of noise and a considerable mess.

## Ducks

A lone duck, presumably blown off course by a storm, sheltered on a corner of our croquet lawn. It stayed with us for two days until it had recovered its strength enough to be able to fly away. On another occasion a visiting duck laid a huge mound of eggs in the rhubarb patch. Sadly, all the eggs were eaten by a fox. The duck escaped though it protected its eggs ferociously and lost quite a number of feathers.

## Alice the healer

Once, I was due to go to Paris for the weekend. I had been looking forward to the trip for weeks. I had been working on a book (as usual) and I was exhausted.

When I arrived at Bristol airport I was told that my flight had been cancelled and that I had to fly from Birmingham instead. I could not bear the thought of a long delay and a trip all the way to Birmingham and so I went back to the car park, retrieved my car, and drove home. When I arrived I found that I could not get into the house because I didn't have a key with me. I sat in the car feeling very sorry for myself. Suddenly, Alice appeared on the bonnet in front of me. I opened the car door and she jumped inside. She sat on my chest, with her paws either side of my neck and purred loudly. I soon felt better.

## Lost and found

When we were living in Lynmouth in Devon I once thought that Alice had completely disappeared. For nearly twenty four hours there was no sign of her. I was desperate and quite beside myself with worry. I am a pessimist by nature and as a writer I have a well developed and rather active imagination. I checked everywhere that she could have been hiding or stuck and I walked round and round the garden and the surrounding woodland calling her name in case she was lying injured somewhere.

Eventually I found her shut in an outside studio where I had been working. She must have sneaked in, unseen, when I had first entered and then found somewhere to hide. When I had left she'd been asleep and had stayed behind. And when I'd first checked the building she must have still been asleep. When I eventually found her the inside of the building was a mess. Alice had ripped up the carpet and clawed at the doors in her attempts to escape. When I finally opened the door she was delirious with delight. I suspect that her purring must have been heard in London.

## Sensitive and susceptible

Cilla, Karen, Septimus and Snowy, the four sheep who live with me, will always run for shelter if the weather is bad. They don't much mind wind but they absolutely hate rain.

*"The sheep do not like the rain."*

Actually, it isn't just bad weather which they dislike. They don't like hot weather very much either. If it is unusually sunny they turn into honorary vampires: at sunrise they go indoors and shelter in the shade and cool of the shippen, and at dusk they come out and graze by moonlight through the night. There is, I suspect, a widespread feeling that sheep are hardy creatures who do not mind being outside whatever the weather. This is simply not true. Sheep are sensitive, susceptible creatures who hate cold or hot weather but who have to put up with it because farmers give them no option by shutting them in open fields. Remember this next time you drive pass a field without shelter where sheep are huddled against a low hedge in a storm. In the wild sheep can take protection among rocks or under trees but farmed sheep cannot usually do either.

## Septimus gets maternal

Every spring several lambs find their way through the hedge into one of our fields. The ewes usually force their way through the hedge to be with their lambs. But one year a particularly persistent lamb managed to get through by itself. Its mother stayed on the other side of the hedge and made a lot of noise.

Septimus adopted the persistent lamb, staying with it, protecting it from danger and generally taking on the role of surrogate mother. It was all rather a surprise. I had never thought of Septimus as having a strongly developed maternal instinct. The lamb stayed with Septimus for two days. I was about to telephone the farmer and ask if I could buy the lamb when, presumably missing its real mother, the lamb left us and went back home through the hedge.

## Faking a limp

Karen, an adorable and charming creature, is not beyond a little occasional manipulation if she feels she is not receiving enough attention. If, for example, she feels that she has not received enough hugs and cuddles she may feign a limp. She knows that if she appears to have a slight limp then she will receive lots of attention. But she also knows that as long as she is careful not to overdo things I will not call the vet straight away.

On several occasions she has had me fooled. I have been worried by what has appeared to be a genuine limp only for the limp to disappear when she has had her cuddles and she thinks I am not looking. I sometimes peep from an upstairs window to see whether or not an apparent limp is genuine.

*"Karen knows that if she appears to have a slight limp she will receive lots of extra attention."*

### "I hate fish!"

Alice's least favourite food was fish. Her second least favourite food was anything on 'special offer'. Very early on in our relationship I discovered that she had some mysterious way of knowing if I ever tried to buy cheap cat food or anything on 'special offer'.

# Fed by hand

While travelling far away from home I met a man and his wife who run a large farm. Each year there are, inevitably, a number of lambs who have to be fed by hand. The farmer's wife told me that her young children were all given the responsibility for this joyful chore. (It is a chore because you have to feed the animals every four hours or so and this means getting up in the middle of the night, trekking across the farmyard with bottles of warm milk and crouching in the straw to feed young lambs. But it is, nevertheless, a joy.)

I asked her what happened to the animals when they were strong enough to graze.

The farmer's wife told me that the animals were then turned out into the fields and allowed to fend for themselves. She admitted, however, that sometimes young lambs which had become particularly loved pets would be allowed to graze on the farmhouse lawn.

I then asked her what happened to the animals when they were older.

The farmer's wife looked at me as though she couldn't understand the question. She told me that the animals were (of course) sent to the abattoir.

I felt sick and had to leave.

And what she told me frightened me.

What sort of people develop from children who are taught to regard lambs as dependent pets - and then taught that it is perfectly acceptable to have them killed when, commercially, the time is right?

I find it hard enough to cope with the sight of thousands of lambs in the fields. I like watching the lambs at play but it upsets me to think of the future which awaits them.


# Alice's Diary

After 'Alice's Diary' was first published people (usually librarians or bookshop assistants) would often ring up and ask us for the name of the 'real' author. (Alice's name is on the copyright line inside the book as well as being on the cover and the title page). For several years we always used to insist that Alice had written the book by herself. All the callers happily accepted this. (It wasn't until quite recently - when a lot of people had already guessed - that we publicly revealed that I had helped Alice with the writing and the illustrating of her books.)

## Creature of habit

Since I am a creature of habit I always used to sit in the same chair in the living room. Alice would rush in, leap onto my lap and settle down without even checking to see that the person in the chair was me. One day a stranger sat in my chair and so I had to sit in another chair on the other side of the fireplace. Alice came rushing into the room as usual and leapt, without looking, onto the stranger's lap. She hated strangers. When she realised what she had done she leapt up as though she was treading on hot coals and raced over to where I was sitting.

*"She hated strangers sitting in 'our' chair."*

## Playing in the spring

If you watch young lambs playing in the fields in spring time you will see that they play many of the same games that human children play. They race each other from one spot to the next - and back again. They play hide and seek. And I have even seen lambs playing tag. Sometimes a lamb will straighten its legs and jump about as though on springs. This is affectionately known as "pronging".

## Goodbye flowers!

When the field in which the sheep normally live was infested with the foot rot germ I put them into the garden for two weeks so that the bug would die and the grass would be clean by the time they returned. The doors to the barn we use as a garage were left open so that they could shelter if it was raining. There was at least an acre of grass for them to eat but they hardly touched any of it. Instead they lunched and dined on flowers, vegetable plants and tree bark.

*"The sheep had been in the garden for two weeks. There wasn't a flower left"*

I had to put wire netting around several dozen trees to stop the sheep doing too much damage. When not eating the four sheep spent much of their time lying on the path directly outside the front door. Whenever the front door was open they did their best to get into the house.

*"Every time we opened the front door the sheep tried to get into the house."*

Since we did not encourage this they got their own back by eating great chunks out of the door and the door frame. I have never heard of other sheep eating doors and gates. Septimus, Snowy, Karen and Cilla have so far damaged at least half a dozen large wooden gates. They completely ate their way through two bars of one five bar gate at my last home. (The whole gate had to be replaced). However, I confess that despite all the damage done to flowers, bushes, trees and the front door I rather liked having them in the garden.

## A tiny drop of blood

One day there a tiny drop of blood on Alice's fur; just at the side of her mouth. I looked into her mouth and could not see anything particularly unusual. There was a black patch on her gum but it had always been there - it was a part of her markings. But I got the vet to see her. The vet didn't think there was anything to worry about. But she arranged for some tests to be done.


## Splash!

When Alice and Thomasina were tiny kittens I put their litter tray in the downstairs lavatory. There was plenty of room and it seemed a good idea to keep all such activities confined to the same part of the house. Neither of them had the foggiest idea what the tray was for and I had to teach them how to dig little holes in the soft earth. I used my fingers and then they followed my example and used their paws. They both quickly realised the purpose of the tiny holes they had dug. Nature then took over.

Since Alice had never known a mother of her own she took me for her mentor in all matters domestic. One day she watched me use the human size lavatory and, in my absence decided that she wanted to follow suit.

She fell in.

I was in my study, quite a distance away, but I heard her anguished cries and rushed and rescued her. When I pulled her, sopping wet, out of the lavatory bowl I dabbed her as dry as I could with a towel and then put her inside my shirt. She was shivering and I was frightened that she would catch cold.

From that day on Alice was the dearest, most loving friend anyone could have. She comforted me, loved me and sat with me when I worked.

When she was small I used to write on an electric typewriter and she quickly found out how to turn on the machine. If I went out for an hour or two I would come back and find the typewriter hum-

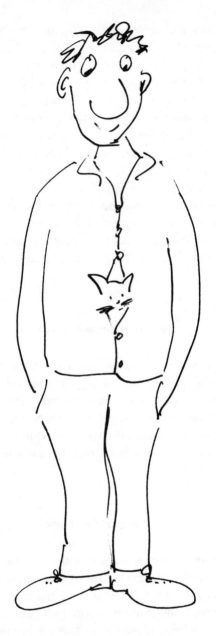

*"I put her inside my shirt until she was dry."*

ming and Alice tucked up beside it. She liked the warmth and she liked the comforting hum. Actually, it was more of a purr than a hum.

The only times she ever got cross with me was if I went away for a few days. (Throughout her life I never went away from her for more than five or six days at a time). Moments after I returned from a trip away she would hurl herself into the room to make sure that I had truly come back and then hurl herself out again before I could say hello. She would then disappear for exactly an hour. Not fifty minutes or an hour and ten minutes but an hour. She would hide outside and she would get very cross and upset if I tried to find her or tried to persuade her to come to me. After an hour, having made clear her displeasure, she would come rushing back into the house and leap onto my shoulder. She would not then leave me for anything. I had to eat, wash and even clean my teeth with her draped around my neck.

## In the summerhouse

In the spring, summer and autumn (and sometimes in the winter too) I would work outside in the garden - either in the summerhouse or on a swing seat or on of the many benches that were scattered about. Alice would always find me and sit with me. She loved the summerhouse. There were two chairs in there. I used to sit on one and she would often sit on the other while I sat with my notebook on my lap and wrote.

## Through the tears

Although I scribbled notes to myself at the time (as though I could ever forget those awful months) I did not, could not, write about Alice's illness and death at the time. I tried to but I just couldn't see my computer screen through the tears. It is now four years since Alice died and I can just about bring myself to write about her final illness.

# Friday the 13th

I have always been particularly superstitious about Friday 13th and so when Alice and I needed to see the vet on Friday 13th March 1992 to receive the results of the tests that had been done I asked the vet to visit us at home. It seemed somehow safer. When the vet came she told us that Alice had cancer. The evil I have always associated with Friday 13th had visited us in our home. I burst into tears when the vet told me that Alice was dying. I was shaking so much with tears and sadness that I couldn't even see the vet to the door.

# Desperately hungry

In the final days Alice was desperately hungry because she couldn't eat properly. Somehow she dragged herself outside and caught a mouse, brought it into the house and killed it. There was blood everywhere - some of it the mouse's and some of hers. But she couldn't eat the creature. (I hate seeing cats kill but it is what they do. It is their nature. And they are of necessity carnivores. I would rather a cat ate a mouse it had killed than that I had to open a can of meat obtained from an abattoir-killed animal). Towards the end Alice could only eat soup. Her favourites were parsnip, tomato and orange and carrot and butterbean. She could not swallow properly and so she dribbled soup all around the house for some time afterwards.

I thought about major surgery and radiotherapy. I would have done anything, given every penny I could raise, to keep Alice alive. I thought about reconstructive surgery. But all that would have been for me and not for her.

# Our last evening

The illness was terrible. Alice couldn't eat properly. And then there was a tooth missing. And because she couldn't swallow properly strings of saliva started to collect around her jaw. There was an operation. In the end Alice could not eat or drink at all. On the evening before she died she would not leave me. I helped her into the airing cupboard (her favourite place) but she would not stay there. She wanted to be with me. She had been dribbling on me all day and so I went for a bath. She came with me. She sat on the edge of my bath and was so thirsty that she tried to drink my bath water. But she couldn't. She was desperately thirsty but she just couldn't swallow. The water just came back out of her mouth.

As she sat on the edge of my bath, we both knew that it had to be our last evening together. I desperately wanted to find a surgeon to try and cure her. But the tumour was too big, too deep, too fast growing and I knew that it was no good. In those last days I wrote to friends that she was 'one of our family' and I truly meant that. Friends who had never prayed before prayed for her and sent loving messages to her. I loved her so much, so very much.

## Alice and the buzzard

Just a few days before her death, when she was very weak, Alice saw a buzzard sitting on one of our gates. She went up to the buzzard, which was facing the other way, and sniffed its tail. The buzzard turned round, looked at Alice for a moment, and then turned back. It did not move for a minute or two. Finally, when it was ready to move, it slowly and gracefully left the gate and flew low over the field. Alice, bemused by the bird, just watched it go.

## Too weak to walk

Towards the end of her life Alice was too weak to go for a walk. She would, however, sit on my shoulder, dribbling blood, while I went for a short walk. One day in early April we went for a walk together and it was slightly windy. She was so light that she nearly blew off my shoulder but I am sure that she obtained pleasure from the sunshine and the companionship. We lived each day for what it could bring. Although she had been ill for longer the final stretch of Alice's illness, after the diagnosis of cancer was made, lasted just one month.

## Goodbye

I knew when the time had come to say goodbye to Alice. For years I had dreaded anything happening to Alice or Thomasina. And then, when I knew that she had cancer, I worried about whether or not I should interfere. Would I, I wondered, be putting her out of her misery? I did not want to make the mistake of putting her out of my misery. People have animals put down because they are messy or inconvenient or because it is distressing to look at them. But none of that is reason enough. Right at the end of her illness I began to hope that Alice would die in her sleep (and so enable me to avoid the awful responsibility for taking the decision I did not want to take). She gave up eating. She could not drink. She was in so much discomfort that there was no quality to her life. I knew the time had come for me to interfere with nature when I awoke and knew that I dreaded finding her still alive. The time had come when I knew that life for her was not worth living; there was no quality in her life. There was just the living and the living alone was not enough; there were no longer any moments of joy or even of contentment, just unremitting, long moments of pain and unhappiness. It was an awful realisation. I wanted her to live for ever for my sake but for her sake I knew I could no longer hold back the final comfort I could offer her. It was the very last thing I could do for her as her friend. And part of the very last thing I could do for her as a friend was to be with her, to hold her, during those final few seconds.

* * * *

The vet had given me an injection to give her when the time was right. But although I tried to give her the injection I couldn't do it. The vet came and while Alice sat peacefully on my lap she injected her with a drug to give her peace. It was my last gift to her. It was, for her, relief from hunger and thirst and pain. I held her as she died and I sat there for some time afterwards; holding her and crying. It was the most difficult thing I have ever done in my life and it took every ounce of courage I could find.

She fell asleep in my arms and I sat with her, tears running down my cheek, stroking her and remembering the good days. My sadness was not so much for her as for me. I felt overwhelmed, numbed, by loneliness. For her I felt relief that she would no longer be in pain. She was beyond evil and pain; untouchable by the vivisectors and the unthinking, the cruel and the barbaric.

I sat with her as she died. I held her close to me and I wept for her. I also wept for me. It was an awesome and dreadful responsibility.

Had I done wrong?

Horace, the Roman poet, wrote: 'To save a man's life against his will is the same as killing him.' Seneca, another Roman writer, said: 'Death is a punishment to some, to some a gift, and to many a favour.' Sophocles, the Greek dramatist, wrote: 'Death is not the greatest of ills, it is worse to want to die, and not to be able to.'

The words echoed around and around.

I weep that she is no longer with me. I mourn for her daily. And every day or so I still ask myself whether or not I did the right thing. But, after years of heart searching I know that I would not, could not, have done things differently. I loved her too much.

## Thoughts on euthanasia

Alice's death made me think hard about euthanasia. Think of an old man. Much older than nine year old Alice. The old man in constant pain. He is marooned, without hope, between life and death. He is brave and courageous and he is dying. The pain is so great that he can not move. He can hardly talk. The pain, the desperation and the anguish are clearly visible in his eyes. Pain is the one thing he has in abundance. He knows that he is dying and he has come to terms with death. He has beaten death because he is not afraid of it. And he has been trying to die for 48 hours. He knows that now is the time to die in peace and with dignity. In his spirit he has beaten death but she, in her spite, will not embrace him. His heart has faltered twice but on each occasion the hospital's emergency resuscitation team has been called into action. White coated specialists, surrounded by bleeping equipment have dragged him back into the land of the living; the land from which he has been so eager to escape. Everyone knows he is ready to die. Everyone knows that for him there is no escape from death. But the system will not allow him to die. The system rules that he must be kept alive. Each time he tries to fade away he is dragged back into our world. His frail body is blasted with so much electricity that it shakes and convulses with the raw power. He is pumped full of stimulants and at the moment when his eyes showed some faint sign of peace - as death approaches - he is denied that comfort with the aid of modern technology.

Should we make him suffer in this way?

Or should we help him to find peace?

What would you do?

Could you bear to see him suffer more?

Or, to ease his pain would you give him an injection of morphine?

And then watch, while, already weak and exhausted, he drifts peacefully into that final sleep. And just before his heart stutters to a final halt for the third time do you reach across the bed and switched off the cardiac monitor so that this time there is no emergency team and no last minute resuscitation?

There are times when a painkiller will hasten a patient's death. What should the doctor do?

Should he withhold the pain relief lest he interfere with the process of dying?

Should he sit, inactive and rosy with self righteousness and let his patient die slowly and with suffering?

As technology enables us to keep one another alive for longer and longer the whole question of euthanasia becomes increasingly urgent.

Euthanasia is no longer a subject we can afford to push into the dark recesses of our minds. And nor is it a subject we can leave to doctors, social workers or politicians.

Euthanasia is a now a subject we must all take seriously.

If you don't think about it today then by tomorrow you may find that others have made all the important decisions for you.

It seems strange that we are allowed to help the animals we love escape from pain and suffering but we are not allowed to help the humans we love escape when they are suffering and in unavoidable pain.

## Tears and an empty heart

For some time after Alice had died I sat there silently, her still body on my knees, with tears pouring down my cheeks and my heart empty. For weeks, months, afterwards I would suddenly burst into tears for no discernible reason. I felt so sad that she was no longer with me. But I knew, in my heart, that she would never leave me. I am crying now as I write this and I have to type faster and faster while I can still see the screen on which these words appear.

Alice and I lived together for nine years and she was my friend, comfort and inspiration for all that time. Even now, four years after her death, I miss her every day. Little things remind me of her. Thomasina, who knows my moods better than I do, has jumped down from my desk onto my lap again. We will sit quietly and remember the joy Alice gave us.

## Karen and the spray

Karen gets a lot of (genuine) trouble with her feet. But she hates having anything done to them. When I saw her limping (genuinely) one day I suspected that she might this time have a flare up of an old condition of hers - foot rot. I have an aerosol can containing an antibiotic which the vet gave me. It is effective against the bug which causes foot rot. I went into the field and set off towards the shippen. Naturally, all four sheep followed me - with Karen bringing up the rear, limping along. When I entered the shippen Cilla, Snowy and Septimus all ran in after me but Karen waited just outside, looking in through the doorway.

*"Karen waited outside, peeping in through the doorway of the barn."*

Hoping that, if my diagnosis was correct, I would be able to treat her where she stood I picked up the aerosol can from a nearby shelf. Karen saw me pick up the aerosol can, knew immediately that this meant she might have to have her foot sprayed, and ran back up the hill into the field. Even though she had a bad foot she managed to run more quickly than I could. She refused to come back to the shippen. And when I walked up the hill towards her she would only let me get close to her when I opened my hands and showed her that I was not carrying the aerosol can.

## Three cats

We have three cats now: Thomasina, Catallus and Chinti.

Catallus is velvety and black and very cuddly. I think he was rather unhappy as a kitten for he is still rather nervous. But he loves being stroked and is the best ripper of wallpaper I have ever known.

Chinti, another refugee who had an unhappy start to life, is silvery grey with a stripe in her tail. She has been described (not within her hearing) as looking a little like a racoon. She spends much of her life in the airing cupboard but is only really happy when she has a lap to lie on. She has a habit of sharpening her claws on wooden doors. She does this with so much ferocity that I fear she must have a particular dislike of doors.

We had recently been away for a short while and went to collect the three cats from the kennels. Thomasina, who is the most sociable of cats, had made a new friend and had clearly become quite attached to the cat in the neighbouring quarters - a lovely cat called Muffin. When Thomasina heard my voice she rushed to the fence and said goodbye to Muffin. She then rushed over to see me. As soon as she had said 'hello' she raced straight into her carrying basket, turned round, curled up and lay down. She then looked at me as if to say: 'Come on, then. Let's go home!' Naturally, when we got home she refused to have anything to do with me for over two hours. Having made her position clear she then relented, and for the rest of the day she wouldn't leave me at all.

# Togetherness

The sheep really do not like the vet. They run away when they see his car. When they see my car - which is a large, blue, four wheel drive vehicle - they either do not move at all or they run towards the gate to greet me. But when they see the vet's car - which is an almost identical, large, green, four wheel drive vehicle - they run away at a ferocious pace.

*"The sheep do not like the vet."*

This is curious for sheep are supposed to be colour blind. If they truly are colour blind then the only other explanation I can think of is that they recognise the difference in engine noise for the vet's vehicle is a diesel driven motor car while mine is petrol driven.

If they are unable to leave the shippen when he enters they huddle together in a dark and distant corner, presumably hoping that he won't notice or them or will get bored, go away and leave them alone.

One day Cilla had a bad foot. I picked her out and led her to a well lit part of the shippen where the vet and his assistant were waiting (the sheep are so large that even if I wanted to try and use brute force on them it would be quite impossible - they are far too large to be forced to do anything they don't want to do).

When the vet drained the abscess on her foot Cilla was obviously in some pain. I was very moved when Karen, her twin sister, walked slowly but deliberately across the shippen, facing, braving and overcoming her personal fears of the vet, and stood beside Cilla, nuzzling her face and clearly giving her comfort, reassurance and love. It was one of the most touching moments I have ever experienced.

*"Karen stood beside Cilla giving her comfort and love."*

Karen is the most nervous of the four sheep. She is extremely sensitive and it must have taken a tremendous amount of courage for her to walk those few yards to be with her sister while the vet performed the small operation.

The operation was over in a minute or two; the pus was released. As Cilla scrambled to her feet the two sheep stood side by side; the one offering comfort and love and the other receiving both with quiet and grateful dignity.

There are still those who insist that animals do not have emotions.

## Septimus in hospital

One day Septimus had a fit. Afterwards she lay down in the shippen and did not want to move. When I put a bowl of water in front of her she emptied the bowl in one long drink. I gave her a little fresh hay while I refilled the bowl. She toyed with the hay but didn't seem very interested. But she drank another bowl full of water. The vet came to see her. He didn't know what was wrong. He suggested that he take her into the veterinary hospital for a few days observation. Would it help, I asked, if they did some blood tests? The vet thought for a moment and then admitted that they could certainly do blood tests but that there was one problem: there are few 'normal' values available for sheep. Farmers do not normally have blood tests performed on their sheep because the laboratory costs would exceed the value of the sheep.

While Septimus was in hospital we visited her every day. We took books to read and biscuits for her to nibble and sat on deckchairs in her room. When she recovered and was well enough to come home the other three sheep were as pleased to see her as she was to see them.

## The badger's visit

I walked past the shrubbery this morning and saw that an animal, probably a badger, had been digging in the earth. There were, holes, clods of earth and daffodil bulbs all over the place. My feeling of excitement and pride was tempered by the thought that some gardeners would probably put down poison to protect their plants against any animal impertinent enough to imagine it had the right to seek food in what they regarded as their domain.

## Thomasina's drinking habits

Thomasina has a glass full of water by the side of her food bowls. The water is changed regularly so that it is always fresh. (She has a glass because a year or two ago she made it clear that she preferred drinking from ordinary glasses to water bowls).

However, she hardly ever touches her own drinking water supply. If the lavatory seat is left up she will try to drink from the lavatory bowl. If there is a dirty puddle of rainwater outside she will drink from it. She will drink from the bird bath, the water butts in the garden and the dirty washing up water.

She also likes to drink from the bath when I am in it. One night she fell in. She scrambled out again within seconds and did not get very wet. But she was very embarrassed about it.

## Alice writes

Turning out an old drawer recently I found this.

Alice had written it, by walking on the keys of my computer, and I had kept it.

edvtxtsqahcvdfefikrk9nglo b.Opht;f='t
=0;.ooooh864rfdrwwwaj1    'j  jc  hj3hrc65uio^O 6tiosyp88-
9ooooooooooooooooooooooooo;khfhbuiylttrkrcfvdverfra5w45wb^G^E^E^
E^E^E^E^E^E^E^E^E^E^E^E^E^E^E^E^E^E^E^E^E^E^E^E^E^E^E^E^E^E^E^E^
E^E^E^E^E^E^E^E^E^E^E^E^E^E^E^E^E^E^E^E^E^E^E^E^E^E^E^E^E^E^E^E^
E^E^E^E^E^E^E^E^E^E^E^E^E^E^E^E^E^E^E^E^E^E^E^E^E^E^E^E^E^E^E^E^
E^E^E^E^E^E^E^E^E^E^E^E^E^E^E^E^E^E^E^E^E^E^E^E^E^E^E^E^E^E^E^E^
E^E^E^E^E^E^E^E^E^E^E^E^E^E^E^E^E^E^E^E^E^E^E^E^E^E^E^E^E^E^E^E^
(the last block of text is where she sat down).

*"All her own work"*

Alice did not manage to print her own work (as Thomasina did). But when she had finished I printed it out to preserved her work for ever. I am glad I did.

## Silly time

Does anyone know, I wonder, why it is that animals (particularly young ones) seem to have a 'silly time' every evening at around 7.00 pm and 7.30 pm? Cats run around the house and lambs gambol around the meadow with particular enthusiasm at that time of the day. (When people are rushing around getting ready to go out to work in the morning I wonder if cats say to each other: 'Have you noticed how Uprights always race around at this time of day?')

75

# Leaning on a gate

I was standing, leaning on a gate, watching the sheep who were sitting in the field. It was a sunny, warm day and they were simply staring into space.

'I wonder what they're thinking about?' I asked George, a friend of mine who has travelled widely and who was staying with us for a few days. 'Do you think sheep ever get bored?'

George didn't answer for a moment. Then he pushed back the faded, green baseball cap he always wears and scratched at his chin. When he spoke he did so quietly and slowly. He does everything slowly. 'I've seen Zulus sit all day without speaking or doing anything; just moving occasionally to get a drink or to relieve themselves,' replied George. 'And in the Far East being able to sit all day and do nothing and think of nothing is regarded as achieving the highest state of being. When the Zulu tribesman or the Buddhist monk sit and stare into space they are not bored. They are simply content.'

I realised that George was right. It is our materialistic, Western culture which has made simple contentment a thing of the past. These days we are taught and encouraged that we must always be doing something, always striving for something else, always thinking of the future and never thinking of the present; always concentrating on tomorrow and never content with today. The human attention span has become so fragmented that television producers and advertisers no longer expect us to watch anything for more than a few minutes.

I remembered a holiday in the Italian countryside, where relaxation is a national sport and where hurry is something people only do when they are in cars or on motorbikes. Each days I saw men sitting for hours outside the local, village cafes. They drank a little, they smoked a little, they talked a little. But mostly they just sat.

The small hotel where I was staying was at the top of a small hill and each day I walked slowly down to the beach to swim, to read and to relax. Half way down the track between the hotel and the beach there was a small whitewashed cottage with a tiny wooden fence in front of it. The cottage had that slightly derelict look about it that is so common in Mediterranean countries where the climate is more forgiving and loose slates and rotten window frames are less likely to fall victim to harsh winter storms.

On my first morning I noticed that a swarthy, middle aged man in a pair of rather baggy grey trousers and a dirty once white vest had begun to paint the small fence. It would, I suppose, have taken the average Englishman half a day to paint the whole fence.

But at lunchtime I saw the painter sitting at a table outside a small cafe near to the beach. He had a glass of red wine in front of him. He stayed there for the rest of the afternoon.

The following morning the man was back at work, painting his fence again. He worked without haste. And the following lunchtime he was back in the cafe where, once again, he spent the rest of the day.

By the end of my fortnight at the hotel, when it was time for me to hurry back to my own work, the fence was still not yet painted. The man had, by my reckoning, at least another week's work in hand.

Who is the wise man? The man who pushes himself hard, lives to work and grabs his moments of peace in annual instalments, when he is almost certainly too exhausted to enjoy them, or the man who takes his annual holidays in daily instalments? Who is wisest, the man who works himself to the bone so that he can earn a fortune and retire at sixty five a wealthy man or the man who takes his retirement as he goes through life?

Now, when I watch the sheep gazing contentedly into space I do not pity them, fearing that they are bored, but instead I envy their contentment.


## Something strange in the storage heater

I hate any sort of cruelty to animals. It took me many years to reconcile my dislike of cruelty to animals with the fact that cats are inveterate and unstoppable catchers and killers. Alice was an enthusiastic killer and Thomasina is quite a killer too. Like most other cats I have ever known both had a habit of bringing mice, shrews, voles and other creatures into the house and then letting them go by accident or design. I have lived with cats for most of my life and so have always lived with mice and other small creatures too. I am convinced that if I had never had a cat I would have had mouseless houses.

On one occasion a mouse which Alice or Thomasina (who knows which?) brought into the house escaped and hid in a night storage heater in my study. The mouse built a nest in the storage heater and duly died there. I was not aware of this until the corpse of the mouse started to cook and to decompose. The smell was so bad that although it was by now mid winter I had to open all the windows and doors in the house. Because the smell was so bad it took quite a while to find that it was coming from the storage heater. I then had to dismantle the heater, remove the cooked and decomposing remains and then reassemble the heater. No workman would touch this job. It took me a day.

## Lap, please

Catallus wouldn't stop clawing at my trousers. He reached up my trouser leg as far as he could, clawing and miaowing. At first I thought he wanted to be escorted to his food. (He often likes to have someone standing near to him as he eats). But he wasn't hungry. Then I thought that perhaps the cat flap was shut and he wanted to go outside. But the cat flap was open and he didn't want to go outside. Eventually, after ten minutes or so of clawing I realised what he wanted and sat down. He immediately jumped up onto my lap and went to sleep.

## All the same

'Sheep have no individual personalities,' said the first man. 'They always have to be in a flock.'

'You're right,' nodded the second man, sagely.

'I agree,' said the third man. '

'Absolutely,' said the fourth.

'If one gets frightened and starts running all the others follow,' said the first man.

'That's true,' said the second man.
'Boo! said a stranger in uniform.
'Run!' yelled the first man.
'Help!' screamed the second man.
'Let's get out of here!' shouted the third man.
'Wait for me,' said the fourth man.

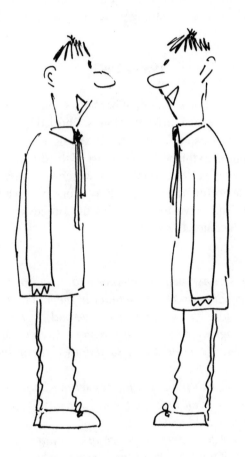

*"Sheep all look the same and have no individual personalities" said the first man. "You're right" said the second man.*

# The leader

Karen is more alert to danger than her twin sister, Cilla, or the other two sheep which whom she lives - Snowy and Septimus. If she suspects any danger she be the first to run away - the others then follow her. It would be easy to assume from this behaviour that Karen is the leader. And that when and where she goes the others follow. This is not the case at all. It is simply that Karen is more sensitive than the others. Her 'leadership' is nothing more than an enhanced sensitivity to danger.

# 1983 - 1992

I buried Alice with copies of both of her books and a favourite jumper of mine which was also a favourite of hers. I buried her next to one of her favourite trees - a spot from which she could watch both the front and back entrances to the house and most of the driveway.

Here is what we wrote on the note which we buried with Alice, in a home made coffin, underneath a gravestone which a local stonemason carved. The gravestone contains the single word Alice and, underneath it, the dates 1983-1992.

*15.5.92*

*This is Alice, a tortoiseshell, mixed tabby cat who was born in April 1983 and collected from a cat sanctuary in the midlands. She was a dear and deeply loved friend; always patient and always affectionate. Her daily greetings were a constant joy. She went to sleep for ever on the 12th May 1992. She died of a squamous cell carcinoma of her lower jaw.*

*Alice wrote two popular and bestselling books - Alice's Diary and Alice's Adventures and had thousands of friends and fans around the world.*

*If you have to disturb Alice we ask that you now allow her to rest in peace; if not here then somewhere nearby.*

### Snowy limps too

I had to travel abroad to see one or two publishers who were interested in publishing some of my books. A few minutes before I was due to leave for the airport I noticed that Snowy was limping a little. I telephoned the friend who was coming to look after the sheep and asked him to keep a close eye on Snowy and to call the vet if she was still limping in another 24 hours. While I was away I telephoned to see how Snowy was. My friend told me that Snowy had been fine. She had run to him with the others. She had limped not at all - except when she had had her biscuit and wanted another. She had, he said, been clearly limping in the hope that she would receive extra sympathy - and an additional biscuit. The sheep are getting very clever. Karen has been aware for some months that limping can be used as a way to obtain extra sympathy. Now that Snowy has learned the same trick life is going to be even more difficult.

## Memoirs of Alice

I remember so many things about Alice. I remember the way she used to jump up and open doors by clinging to the handle. I remember the way she used to claw at the door and carpet if she couldn't open a door - creating absolute havoc.

I remember the way she used to follow me up the lane if I set off on my bicycle or even in the car. At the top of the lane (on the far edge of her territory) she would sit and watch me disappear with a sad look on her face. She never went further than the top of the lane.

*"Alice would sit and watch me dissappear with a sad look on her face."*

82

I remember her poking her head through the cat flap when it was snowing and staying there for over a minute, watching the snow flakes fall, her head protected by the cat flap. She would do the same thing if it was raining; using the flap as an umbrella.

I remember the first time she went out into the snow. After every step she would shake each paw to get rid of the snow flakes.

I remember the way she would walk on my computer keyboard and then look at me, expecting me to be pleased with her for having been so helpful.

## My nightmare

I have a recurring nightmare from which I always awake in a sweat. In the nightmare I am in a laboratory, handcuffed and chained to a pillar so that I cannot move. Two yards in front of me a white coated scientist is performing an experiment on a tabby cat. The cat is clearly alive and alert but is strapped into a metal and leather contraption so that he or she cannot move. Electrodes are attached to shaved areas of the cat's skull and chest and lead to an instrument with a couple of dials on the front of it. The scientist has drilled a hole in the cat's skull and a thin piece of red rubber tubing emerges from the hole. Using a glass pipette the scientist drops several millilitres of a clear fluid directly into the cat's brain. I feel nauseated. The cat screams in agony and struggles to free itself. But it cannot. The shock is so great that the cat urinates and defaecates involuntarily. The screams die down into a pitiful, soft miaow. The scientist studies the two dials in front of him and calmly makes a note of the readings. He takes no more notice of the cat than he takes of the table upon which he is writing. The cat is just another piece of equipment. The bile rises in my throat and I feel myself retching. My body's spasms are restrained by the chains around me. And then the scientist turns the framework holding the cat and I can see the animal's face. It is Alice. I can see the pain in her eyes. There is only one message there. 'Help. Please do something.' That is my night-time nightmare. My daytime, waking nightmare is that every cat in every laboratory everywhere in the world is another Alice.

# A slight weight problem

Septimus isn't lazy, and given the right incentive she can run faster than I can, but she has what must rather bluntly be described as something of a weight problem and she doesn't like walking more than is necessary.

She has developed a peculiar habit of snacking while sitting down; nibbling away at every blade of grass within reach. When she has eaten all the grass within range and has to move a yard or two to find another dining area she leaves behind a crescent shaped patch of neatly mown grass, chewed right down to the ground.

She and her three friends were in the garden one day when I had to go down to unfasten the padlock on the gate so that a visitor I was expecting could get in. So that they wouldn't all follow me to the front gate I tried to sneak around the back of the house, past the barn which serves as a garage and then down the narrow path through the small bluebell wood.

But Snowy spotted me and with a loud baaa quickly alerted the rest. She, Cilla and Karen chased around the back of the house and followed me. Because I didn't want them trying to pick a way through the small wood and getting stuck in the brambles (the sheep are, I fear, too wide for the narrow path) I decided to follow the driveway down to the gate instead.

At the bottom of the drive I looked behind me. Snowy, Cilla and Karen were wandering along cheerfully like children on a school outing but there was no sign of Septimus. I then looked up the hill and saw her standing on the lawn outside the front of the house, carefully watching what was going on.

She had clearly guessed where I was heading. And when she decided that her guess was right and she knew exactly where I was going she leapt off the lawn, trotted through the strawberry bed and picked her way carefully down a path along the side of the hedge which divides the garden from our main field. It was a very effective short cut. She arrived on a bend in the driveway just as I did - and a full half minute before her three friends got there.

Snowy, Cilla and Karen baaaed at her a lot (I think they thought that she had cheated) but Septimus just stood there looking very pleased with herself.

## Alice will live forever

Although Thomasina liked to play while Alice was more of a dreamer Thomasina was always rather shy compared to Alice.

*"Thomasina liked to play but Alice was more of a dreamer."*

If they decided that it was time for them to be fed (or they wanted to show me something) they would both come up to my study. Thomasina would sit outside in the corridor, waiting, while Alice would leap up onto my lap, shoulders and desk, making it perfectly clear that she wasn't going to leave me alone until I took notice of her. If I tried to finish the sentence I was writing she would wander up and down the keyboard or lie down on top of the screen and let her bushy tail hang down and swish about so that I couldn't see what I was writing. Thomasina is rather more subtle. If she wants to be fed she will come and sit beside me. I will make my lap available. But she will ignore the offer. I know then what she wants.

Every day I find it difficult to believe that Alice is dead; that she will never again jump onto my shoulders just as I strip off to get into the bath (ouch!) and that she will never again run up the driveway to meet me, her tail held high.

But Alice will live for ever in my heart, in the hearts of all those who were privileged to know her and, I hope, in the hearts of those who read her books.

## The foot bath

The vet suggested that in order to harden the sheeps' feet, and thereby reduce their chances of developing foot problems, we should persuade them to stand in or walk through a formalin foot bath.

I purchased a huge drum of formalin from the veterinary hospital, brought it home and with the aid of an enormous piece of black plastic, a number of spare roofing slates and a stone drainage channel already built into the floor of the shippen, I built a foot bath.

Wearing Wellington boots I then walked through the formalin footbath with a large box containing biscuits. I sat down with both hands full of biscuits and called the sheep.

When the sheep arrived and saw me and the biscuits they were very keen to come to me. But they were not keen enough to walk through the formalin bath. They simply do not like getting their feet wet.

*"They simply do not like getting their feet wet"*

(When they were much smaller they had to be carried through the mud outside the stable. I eventually laid a long paving slab path so that they could reach their stable without having to walk on any muddy ground).

So, there we were. Stalemate. Me on one side of the formalin footbath. And the four sheep on the other side.

Eventually, the temptation proved too much for Septimus. She raced through the footbath so quickly that I very much doubt whether the formalin could possibly have had any useful effect. A moment or two later Snowy followed her example. Neither Cilla nor Karen would venture through.

But I have had my feet in the formalin. Both my Wellington boots had holes in them.


## Whoops!

Thomasina occasionally suffers from slight bladder problems. These do not last more than a few hours but result in her urinating in unusual places - often on the carpet. One day she had one of her attacks and chose to urinate in a large cardboard box full of papers. She has never done this before. The papers in the box were all letters from organisations complaining about my books and articles attacking animal cruelty! I'm not surprised that she could not tell the difference between this correspondence and a litter tray for I am often tempted to make the same mistake myself. Tragically, I have had to throw away all the correspondence.


## What I have learnt

The animals who have shared my life have taught me so much. I have learnt from them the certainty that each and every animal is unique; that animals are emotionally labile, intelligent and sensitive and that they feel anxiety, sorrow and happiness just as much as I do.

## Vive la différence!

When Alice was alive Thomasina would never sit draped around my neck. She never even tried, although we had a close and loving relationship. She was content to sit on my lap. But the day after Alice died Thomasina jumped, very uncertainly, onto my neck. She clung there precariously. She became fairly adept at clinging on while I walked about but I don't think she ever really liked it; and she never thoroughly mastered the trick. She wobbled a good deal and never looked or felt very stable. Now she has given up trying. In a way I am glad. Thomasina and Alice are quite different and I love them both for who they are.

## Happy birthday

I celebrated the sheeps' fifth birthdays by giving them biscuits and singing Happy Birthday' to each of them in turn. They seemed to enjoy the biscuits more than the singing - which shows what good taste they have.

*"I celebrated the sheeps' birthday by singing 'Happy Birthday' to them."*

## Ouch!

When I went into the field Karen was charging around and around as though she was having a fit. I chased after her and we careered around the field like children playing tag. I couldn't get anywhere near to her. I couldn't help thinking that if only she had been able to hold a ball she would have been a valuable member of any rugby side. Eventually, I realised that she had a large piece of dead bramble stuck to her wool - and one free end of the bramble was sticking into her bottom. I couldn't catch her to remove the bramble but eventually I managed to get close enough to put one foot on the other end of the bramble and it tore away from her wool quite easily. Karen, instantly relieved, then stood still and let me give her a cuddle.

## A walk in the wood

Thomasina and I went for a walk through our wood. After three quarters of a mile or so she got tired and let me know that she wanted to ride the rest of the way. I bent down so that she could leap up into my arms. After a couple of hundred yards I felt her body stiffen and then I could feel her tensing ready to jump down to the ground. I bent down so that she wouldn't have so far to jump (I am well over six foot tall) and then I saw what she had seen: a badger. The badger was standing no more than twenty or thirty yards away from me. As soon as Thomasina hit the ground she started running. I ran after her, worried about what would happen if she decided to get too friendly with the badger (or if she foolishly and uncharacteristically tried to pick a fight with it). The badger then ran off through the thick grass and disappeared a moment or two later. Thomasina stood still and stared, and then turned and looked at me. She looked very pleased with herself.

# The duckling

I was in Paris. It was a beautiful spring day and I was relaxing by the river Seine. Suddenly I noticed a pair of ducks swimming along towards me. They weren't so much swimming as floating because they were allowing the river to move them along. Occasionally they stopped and either tipped themselves heads down bottoms up in that smooth way that ducks have or nibbled at something on the bank. Behind them floated half a dozen tiny, closely grouped fluffy ducklings all quack quack quacking and splashing away for all they were worth. They bumped into one another, deliberately and accidentally, and they tried to climb out onto the bank and fell back into the water and they generally misbehaved and had a wonderful time as they floated along in the spring sunshine. And a couple of feet behind the group of ducklings there came a solitary, rather lonely looking little duckling. Every now and again he tried to catch up with the group of ducklings and join in the fun. But every time he did catch up the other ducklings turned on him, attacked him, pecked him and started to make such a dreadful racket that the two parent ducks turned round, saw what was happening, and joined in the attack. Horrified, I started to walk along the bank beside this drama and watched as the two adult ducks, aided and abetted by their infant brood, tried to drown what was clearly a duckling who had got parted from his true family and was now lost. Time and time again the duckling, bedraggled and weakened by the constant batterings he was receiving, drifted away from the family group. And time and time again he paddled back and attempted to win acceptance. It was heartbreaking. At one point, quite exhausted by the battering he was receiving, he climbed out onto the bank to rest. It was a huge struggle for him. I gently tried to persuade him to walk up stream, in the hope that he would be able to find and rejoin his own real family group. But he didn't want to go upstream. He wanted to go downstream, to follow the family he was trying to join. The wrong family. In a clumsy, out of water flurry of downy feathers he tumbled back into the river and continued his attempts to join the family which didn't want him. As the group drifted out of sight the battle was still continuing.

In any society there are outsiders, doomed to remain unwanted and unloved through no fault of their own. In the animal kingdom at large the greatest examples of unkindness (as opposed to death and destruction) are usually directed at those who are members of the same species. Ours is the only species which routinely and deliberately treats all other species cruelly and without compassion.

## The baby rat

Catallus brought a baby rat into the kitchen. The rat was not about to give up its life without a fight. It stood on its hind legs and screamed. Every time Catallus approached it screamed louder. Catallus eventually decided that the whole thing was far too much trouble. He jumped up onto the table, curled up and went to sleep. It took me ten minutes to persuade the rat to leave the kitchen and go into the boot room. There is a cat flap in the door from the boot room to the conservatory and to my astonishment the rat leapt through this flap as though he had been doing forward rolls through vertically swinging doors all his life. He then escaped to the outside world by diving through the cat flap in the outside conservatory door.

## Hunt the hay

It was raining. I went into the shippen and put down some fresh straw for the sheep to lie on. As always they started to hunt through the mounds of fresh straw looking for tasty bits worth eating. (I had just refilled their hay rack but they didn't seem to be interested in that). They didn't seem to find much worth eating amidst the piles of straw. So I had an idea. I grabbed several handfuls of sweet, fresh, hay from the hay rack and stuffed these handfuls of hay into the mounds of straw. The sheep were terribly excited when they discovered these mouthfuls and played 'hunt the hay' for quite some time.

*"The sheep played 'hunt the hay' for quite some time."*

## Checkpoint Charlie

The door from the kitchen into the front hall marks an important boundary zone in our house. It is our feline Checkpoint Charlie. Catallus and Chinti live in the kitchen, the boot room, the boiler room, the dairy and the conservatory. Thomasina lives in the rest of the house. We have to keep the cats apart because Chinti and Catallus (and Chinti in particular) seem determined to kill poor Thomasina.

For some weeks after they all met we tried to encourage the three cats to be friends. Eventually we decided that although Catallus would probably become accustomed to sharing the house with Thomasina there was no chance of Chinti ever becoming used to the idea. She is very jealous and since Thomasina is a much smaller, lighter, older cat we are frightened that Chinti might seriously hurt her. On several occasions we had to drag Chinti away by force. And now, of course, Chinti has become obsessed with the door - and what is on the other side of it. She spends much of her day crouched by the door, her nose to the tiny space between the bottom of the door and the carpet.

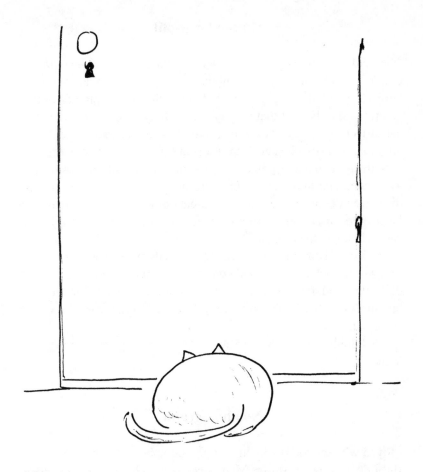

*"Chinti has become obsessed with the door and what is on the other side of it."*

Even more bizarre is the fact that Thomasina spends much of her day crouched on her side of the door. She would run a mile if the door was opened but with an inch of so of thick wood between her and Chinti she seems full of curiosity. Visitors who do not have cats living in their homes with them find this a strange way to live. Visitors who understand and care for cats do not find our Checkpoint Charlie in the slightest bit odd.

# Abused for profit

The fields are full of ewes and new born lambs. Some of the fields are crammed with far too many animals with the result that sheep and lambs are forced to graze on soiled grass. Sheep are quite fastidious creatures and the fact that they eat grass doesn't mean that they will eat dirt - or worse. For example, Snowy, Septimus, Karen and Cilla all adore digestive biscuits but if a small piece of biscuit is dropped onto the ground and becomes slightly muddy none of them will eat it. The sheep and lambs who are overcrowded and forced to graze on dirty ground must suffer greatly. I dream of a day when animals will be treated kindly and compassionately and not abused in this way solely in the name of profit.

There is another problem for animals when they are packed together in such overcrowded conditions: it can become exceedingly difficult for a lamb and its mother to become reunited when there are hundreds of other lambs and ewes all lost and crying for one another at the same time.

I doubt if many farmers appreciate or worry about these problems.


# No photograph!

I toyed with the idea of including photographs of Alice in this book. But I decided not to do so. Many readers who have enjoyed her two books will have their own ideas of what Alice looks like. And I think it is best that they think of her and remember her as the cat they imagined. Photographs aren't necessary. A photograph merely indicates a physical likeness. And there is more, far more, to the one we love than a physical likeness. I wanted to include pictures of Alice that captured just a little something of her spirit. And so, I have included in this book drawings of Alice which, I hope, will do just that.

# Thank you!

Thank you for allowing me to share my memories of Alice with you and for enabling me to introduce you to my other animal friends.

# Afterword

# How Alice Changed My Life

*[Note: I am advised by those whose advice I usually take that this section should not appear here - at least not without a good deal of cutting. It should, I am told, appear in my autobiography. I am, however, rejecting good advice and including these paragraphs in Alice and other Friends. It was solely through Alice that I became a publisher and therefore this abbreviated story of my publishing experiments belongs here.]*

Alice changed my life in several very important ways.

I had always been opposed to the use of animals in scientific experiments, regarding vivisection as a barbaric and pointless activity, but I had been so involved in the campaigns I had run on behalf of people that for some years I had not spent as much time as I should have done campaigning against animal experimentation. I had written scathingly about researchers of all kinds (including those performing animal experiments) when I wrote my second book, 'Paper Doctors', back in 1976 but animal abuse had not been a primary target for my pen.

Alice changed that.

I realised one day how lucky I was to have met Alice and how awful it would have been if, instead of coming to live with me, she had somehow found her way into a vivisector's laboratory. The thought of Alice strapped into a harness in a laboratory while a scientist sewed up her eyelids or injected chemicals into her brain was for me a living nightmare.

It is not widely realised but vivisectors around the world use thousands of former pets. Domestic cats and dogs are picked up out of the streets and sold to vivisectors who like using them because they are more trusting and less likely to bite than animals which have not grown up in loving human company. The thought of Alice being kidnapped, sold to a laboratory and used as experimental material was almost too awful to bear.

Gradually, during the 1980s I began to spend more and more of my life campaigning for animal rights. That was the first way in which Alice changed my life.

It was because I was terrified of Alice and her half sister Thomasina being run over (or, indeed, kidnapped by vivisectors - a much greater problem than is generally realised) that I moved to a house in the country - well away from a public road. In the country I watched lambs playing in the fields and realised that they played just the same sort of games as young children. I realised that they, like Alice, had thoughts and emotions and rights. As a city dweller and a scientist I had never before been exposed to the idea that eating animals might be wrong. My medical training had convinced me (as it convinces most doctors) that eating animals was essential for my very survival and continued good health.

And so it was Alice who led to my giving up eating meat.

It was also Alice who was responsible for my starting to publish my own books.

By the mid 1980s, I felt that I knew Alice well enough to write a book with her. And so together we produced 'Alice's Diary' - the memoirs of a cat. At the time it was unusual for me to write a book without having found a publisher. My agent usually arranged a contract before I started to write. But this book was different: I felt I had to write it, but since I wasn't quite sure how it was going to turn out I didn't think there was much point in trying to find a publisher to commission it.

When I'd finished the book I felt it needed illustrating. I knew exactly what sort of drawings I wanted but I didn't know an illustrator I could trust to draw Alice and Thomasina. So I did the drawings myself.

When the book was finished the typescript started a long and fruitless journey around London. Publisher after publisher turned it down.

'This isn't the sort of book Vernon usually writes' 'Is it intended for children or adults?' 'Who is going to buy it?' 'I don't understand it' and (my favourite) 'Vernon doesn't write cat books' were just some of the comments.

After a year or two it was clear that no one wanted to publish 'Alice's Diary'.

I felt certain that there was a market.

And so Sue Ward (who now manages the blossoming empire at Publishing House) and I published it ourselves. I deliberately didn't put my name on the cover.

Within a very short time we had sold over 10,000 hardback copies of 'Alice's Diary' - big enough sales to have put the book into the bestseller lists for many weeks if we had been a 'proper' publishing company.

Despite the misgivings of the professional publishers in London there clearly were people who wanted to read a book written by a cat. At the time I remember being rather pleasantly surprised that we were right and they were all wrong. These days I so expect the 'professionals' to be completely out of touch with what the reading public really wants that I would be worried if I thought I had written a book which any London publisher would want to put on his or her list.

Readers started buying additional copies for friends (I remember that quite early on one reader ordered eleven copies to give away as presents) and Alice started to receive fan mail.

The next book we published was 'Toxic Stress'. I had never had much difficulty in selling medical book ideas to publishers but somehow I knew that this book would never make an orthodox publisher sit up and take notice. I didn't even offer the typescript to any ordinary publishers. The success of 'Alice's Diary' had given me confidence and I had discovered that I much enjoyed having total control of the publication process. Without editors or marketing men to interfere publishing is a real joy.

'The Village Cricket Tour' - a novel describing the adventures of a cricket team on tour around the west country - came next. I can't remember why I decided to write that book. It probably just happened. I always have several dozen book ideas jostling for attention and this one just managed to clamber to the front of my brain and demand to be written next. I remember that the initial print run was 5,000 copies and early on in the book's history most of these were stored in a barn.

I remember Sue's father looking at the rather frightening piles of books and asking me if I thought I might have printed too many.

It wasn't long before readers of 'Alice's Diary' wanted to know if Alice was going to write another book. And so, in 1992, the same year as 'The Village Cricket Tour', along came 'Alice's Adventures'.

Over the years I have dedicated quite a number of books to animals. This book carried the following dedication:

'Dedicated in sorrow to the memory of the thousands of cats and kittens who have died alone, in pain, in fear and without purpose in vivisection laboratories; in hope for the thousands more who wait, frightened and alone in cages; and in thanks to the many Uprights who are fighting to stop this cruel, pointless and inexcusably barbaric practice.'

* * * *

In 1994 I wrote a book entitled 'Betrayal of Trust' - a book which I regarded as one of the most important books I had ever written. 'Betrayal of Trust' was an extended version of a special report called 'Why Doctors Do More Harm Than Good' which I had written for the European Medical Journal and which had been published in paperback form in 1993.

'Why Doctors Do More Harm Than Good' had been reprinted several times, had sold several thousand copies and had attracted a considerable amount of media attention. In one three day period alone I remember doing around twenty local radio interviews.

But the reviewers all ignored 'Why Doctors Do More Harm Than Good' because it was a small, very cheap paperback. And so during 1993 and 1994 I worked on a considerably extended version of the book to be called 'Betrayal of Trust'. I wanted some review coverage because I felt that the message contained within the book was an extremely important one. I felt that 'Betrayal of Trust' was a double edged book. I regarded it primarily as an attack on the medical profession and the pharmaceutical industry (and the dependence of the former on the latter) but also as an animal rights book since it contained the names of dozens of drugs which are sold to doctors to prescribe for patients but which are known to cause extremely serious problems (such as cancer) when given to animals. I felt then (and still believe) that the book provided the evidence which proved once and for all that animal experiments are of no scientific value, making it crystal clear that drug companies use animal experiments as a double edged tool. If, when a drug is tested on animals, there are no signs of any problems the drug company will enthusiastically use the experiments as proof that the drug is safe. On the other hand if the animal tests show that there are problems - for example, because the drug causes cancer, heart disease or kills the animal - the drug company will completely ignore the tests on the grounds that animals are quite different to human beings.

I sent 'Betrayal of Trust' to just about every publisher I could think of. No one was prepared to publish it. Some said the style was too 'popular'. Other publishers used the excuse that the book was too 'academic'. I rather suspected that no one wanted to publish the book because they were frightened that it might annoy the medical and scientific establishment too much.

So, with the success of 'Alice's Diary' and the other self publishing ventures behind me, I decided to publish 'Betrayal of Trust' myself. I didn't care whether or not it made money. I didn't even mind if it lost money. I just felt that the message it contained was so important that the book had to be published. The commercial and financial success of 'Alice's Diary' made it much easier to take this decision and so once again Alice had affected my life. If I hadn't published 'Alice's Diary' I doubt if 'Betrayal of Trust' would ever have been published.

I had published 'Alice's Diary' and the other fiction books I had written under the Chilton Designs imprint but although I had published 'Toxic Stress' under this imprint I didn't feel that 'Betrayal of Trust' would fit comfortably alongside the growing collection of novels - which by now, also included a series of novels about a fictitious Devon village called Bilbury.

The quarterly journal I had founded a year or two earlier (and which was circulating throughout the world in both English and German, but far from breaking even financially) was called the 'European Medical Journal' and so I decided to publish 'Betrayal of Trust' as a

European Medical Journal book.

'Betrayal of Trust' has so far been reprinted three times and there are now around six thousand copies in print. The book hasn't made any money and hasn't covered the initial research costs but it doesn't cost me much money to keep in print and I intend to keep it in print for as long as I possibly can.

\* \* \* \*

Early on I approached a solicitor and asked him to try to arrange for the European Medical Journal and the associated book publishing operation to be turned into a proper charity. I even planned to donate all my other book royalties to the charity in order to give it a constant income.

To my disappointment I discovered that I could not turn EMJ Books into a charity. The main problem, I understand, was the fact that the publishing programme was regarded as having 'campaigning' overtones.

The fact that I couldn't run the EMJ publishing operation as a charity (together with the fact that heavy legal expenses led to the temporary closing of the European Medical Journal) resulted in my decision to take personal financial responsibility for all the EMJ Books I was planning to publish and to bring them within my general publishing activities.

The first commercially successful book which I published under the EMJ imprint was 'Food for Thought', a book which had originally been written as part of a series of books I had agreed to write for one of the world's largest publishers.

The publishers and I disagreed about the content of 'Food for Thought'. They felt that the book was too controversial, too opinionated and contained too much of an attack on meat. They wanted me to change the text. I disagreed with them and wanted to keep the book as it was. In the end I asked them if I could keep the book and abandon the contract. They agreed.

Since then 'Food for Thought' has, despite being a campaigning book, proved to be a huge commercial success. It reprinted five times in the first twelve months and was our first official 'bestseller'.

It has, indeed, been the financial backbone of the EMJ Books imprint.

* * * *

When I was a boy I frequently read with admiration about the relationship between authors and publishers. An author and a publisher would stay together for life in what was more like a marriage than a commercial partnership. But by the time I started writing books the world of publishing had changed irrevocably. The first big change was that editors started moving about between publishing houses. Authors found themselves having a book commissioned by one enthusiastic editor and aided through the editorial production process by a second editor. The book would then be brought into the world by a third editor who might, or might not, like the author or his work. The old fashioned, cosy relationship between publisher and author had changed for ever.

The second big change was that the salesmen and the marketing directors took over the world of publishing. It seems to me that editors no longer have control over which books they will publish. The traditional publishing image of a wise, well read man in a tweed jacket helping an author to turn his raw pages into a good book - and then helping to create an oeuvre - has been out of date for decades. Publishing is now controlled by marketing men in smart suits. They want more of what is already selling and they panic when they realise that the market is saturated with to much of the same. The marketing men tell the editors what to commission. The editors then find an author and tell him to write a book he doesn't particularly want to write. The result, inevitably, is a book without passion which fails to excite the readers. Most of the people in the publishing industry are scared stiff by the very thought of innovation. They prefer to imitate.

Thanks to Alice and her two books I am now convinced that self publishing is the purest form of publishing available to an author. I believe that in the future the large publishing houses which traditionally and currently dominate the literary world will simply produce the books which the marketing men believe will sell in the largest quantities. In the future real books - written from the heart,

102

with passion and with no thought of commercial purpose - will have no future place in the large publishing house. Only authors who are prepared to publish their own work will see truly original, creative, uncommissioned work in print.

The great beauty of having my own publishing company is that I can write the books I want to write - and then worry later about how to sell them. Most of the books I have chosen to write would not have been published by a modern publishing conglomerate. And yet most of the books I have chosen to write and publish have been reprinted (some of them many times) and have sold well. Many of our books would have been on the best-seller lists if we had sold more through the bookshops (where the official best-seller lists are created) and less through the post direct to readers.

* * * *

When I used to write for big publishers just about every book I ever published involved a battle. It took years to find someone brave enough to publish 'Bodypower'. Publisher after publisher insisted that there was no market for such a book. And yet 'Bodypower' went straight into the Sunday Times Top Ten and the Bookseller bestseller list and has never been out of print since. It has been translated into over a dozen languages and extracts from it have appeared in scores of newspapers and magazines around the world. I have made several television series and a radio series based on it.

When the original paperback version of 'Bodypower' went out of print a mass market paperback house bought the rights. Their edition went out of print before it was even published. I took the rights back and sold the book to another publisher. When they, in turn, remaindered their version I bought up all their stock (around 2,000 copies), gave them away and published my own European Medical Journal version. As I write this it is eighteen months since we took back the rights to 'Bodypower' and we now have 10,000 copies of our edition in print (most of them sold).

When I first wanted to write a book about tranquilliser addiction just about every publisher in London told my agent that there was no market for such a book. Publishers told my agent that there was no demand for such a book. When a publisher eventually commissioned 'Life Without Tranquillisers' they wanted major changes making. I refused to make the changes and so we took the book away and eventually sold it to another publisher. The book went straight into The Sunday Times Top Ten the minute it came out. I remember that someone rang the Sunday Times to find out why the book had gone into the bestseller list. 'Because it is so selling so quickly,' was the logical reply.

I could fill a book with stories like this. For example, 'People Watching' (a huge success) was turned down by many publishers. I have very little respect for modern editors and publishers. They live in an enclosed world in London and seem to me to have very little idea of what the world wants to read. Literary editors are, it seems to me, even worse!

\* \* \* \*

In an attempt to find an American distributor for our books I went to the London Book Fair. I also wanted to have a look around to see what the 'big boys' were doing. While I was there I was rather depressed. Everywhere I looked publishers seemed to be doing exactly the same things. There was a 'follow the leader' air to the whole dismal business. I remembered why I had lost faith and interest in traditional publishing companies, and had been inspired to start publishing my own books.

When I left the book fair, which was held in Olympia, I walked back to Paddington Station to catch the train, through Kensington Gardens. By the time I reached the station I had cheered up. I had realised that the fact that most big publishing companies are still playing 'follow the leader' (without really knowing who the leader is, or where they are heading) was excellent news for a small, innovative and daring publishing company.

And it is not all gloom. I recently visited a literary agent in another country. He is keen to sell European Medical Journal books to publishers in his country. He has a cat living in his office whom he found in the street, starving. He has a cat and two dogs at his home. He found them starving in the streets too. It is always a joy to find another human being who loves animals. I am delighted that he is representing my books in his country.

* * * *

So far I have published over thirty of my own books - in a very short space of time. I have found it far more enjoyable than writing books for traditional publishing companies. I can write exactly what I want to write with no interference. I use the profits I make from the current books to pay for new books. Having my own publishing company means that I can publish the books I wanted to write, quickly and without any outside interference. A traditional publisher will usually take between 12 and 24 months to turn a manuscript into a published book. Books which are likely to annoy the establishment or attract legal opposition are often unpublished.

The speed with which the publishing house can operate is important to me. Sue and the staff at Publishing House turned the typescript of 'Power over Cancer' into a book in just five weeks. Since 140,000 a people a year die of cancer in Britain alone and I believe that this book, which names the foods and other triggers which are believed to cause 80% of all cancers, could save four out of five of those deaths it is clear why I felt that speed was essential.

* * * *

One big problem we do have is that as a small publishing company we have a tremendous amount of difficulty in trying to persuade bookshops to take our books. We offer a very good discount and we pay to have the books posted to the bookshops. In addition we take back any book which a bookshop orders and then decides it doesn't want. This means that bookshops take no risk and have absolutely nothing to lose. They can order our books without any risk whatsoever. We spend a fortune on advertising but despite this bookshops are extremely unwilling to take our books unless they have been ordered specifically by a customer.

One bookshop once telephoned on a Monday to order a copy of 'Alice's Diary' for a customer. We accepted the order (on credit) and posted the book. On the following day they rang again and ordered another copy of the same book. We accepted their order and

105

posted a second book. On the Wednesday they rang again. This time they had two orders for 'Alice's Diary'. We posted them two books. When they rang on the Thursday to order another copy we asked if they would like to take a few copies on sale or return. We said that this would enable them to have a better discount, it would mean that they would be able to supply their customers immediately and, if they put the books on their shelves, it might mean that they would sell a few additional copies. They did not think that this was a good idea. And so we sell many of our books by mail order.

Even more frustrating as far as we are concerned are those bookshops who insist that our books simply do not exist. We regularly get telephone calls from would be purchasers who tell us that they have visited every bookshop for miles around and been told that 'Alice's Diary' (or whatever other title they are asking for) does not exist. All our books are listed on computers, microfiche and in every reference book we can find; we sell thousands of books and advertise widely, regularly and expensively. And still there are bookshops who insist that our books don't exist.

* * * *

I run my publishing imprints rather in the way that I believe old fashioned publishers used to operate. I write books which I want to write (rather than books which I know will be commercially successful). Once the book is written I then worry about how to sell it. And at the end of the financial year I hope that the books which sell well will earn enough to subsidise the books for which there is not such a clear market.

I believe that there are only three reasons to do anything: to try to change the world, to have fun and to make money. Sometimes it is possible to do things which satisfy all these three objectives. More often the success of one objective means that one is more capable of pursuing another objective. (So, for example, making money doing something which is dull may enable you to enjoy an experience which is fun.) Only very occasionally is it really possible to combine two of these reasons.

The books which best satisfy all three objectives are the two books I wrote with Alice. Both 'Alice's Diary' and 'Alice's Adven-

106

tures' were fun to write and illustrate. Both have made money and helped to subsidise the research and production of other books. And both may, I hope, help change the world a little by encouraging people to think more about animals as thinking, sensitive creatures instead of objects.

\* \* \* \*

Today, at Publishing House we do not employ anyone who hunts, supports hunting, supports vivisection or approves of any other form of cruelty to animals. Alice introduced me to publishing. It was her first book ('Alice's Diary') which started my whole publishing venture. I now feel a responsibility to her to ensure that we continue to publish books which will tell the truth about animals. We do not (knowingly) sell any of our books to hunters, vivisectors or others who are cruel to animals. As often as possible we make it clear that we do not want such people as customers. We do not advertise in magazines which seem likely to attract the sort of people who hunt. I sincerely wish that more people would follow a similar policy. Those who are deliberately cruel to animals should be isolated from the rest of society.

Finally, I will end this short account of the publishing company which Alice helped to create with a true story about the books which Alice most directly inspired.

Stocks of 'Alice's Diary' and 'Alice's Adventures' were both stored in a barn for some years. When I moved the stock to a new and larger warehouse I discovered that mice had eaten the covers and spines of some of the books.

Alice would have been furious if she had known.

Vernon Coleman 1996

# Alice's Diary £9.95

Over 16,000 delighted readers from around the world have already bought this wonderful book which tells of a year in the life of a mixed tabby cat called Alice. She records the year's events and disasters with great humour and insight and at long last gives us a glimpse of what it is really like to be a cat! Delightfully illustrated throughout, *Alice's Diary* is an absolute must for animal and cat lovers everywhere.

Our files are bursting with letters from confirmed fans who write and tell us how much they have enjoyed this book.

**"I bought Alice's Diary which was read and re-read by young and old members of my family and greatly enjoyed."**
(E. M., Cheshire)

**"I felt I must put paw to paper to say how very much my human and myself enjoyed your Diary."**
(The W family in West Sussex)

**"Alice's Diary is one of the nicest books I have ever read. She has wonderful insight"**
(Mrs J., London)

**"I am delighted with Alice's Diary - I must have Alice's Adventures."**
(V. H., Grimsby)

**"It is a delightful book and I thoroughly enjoyed it."**
(M.E., Sunderland)

# Alice's Adventures £9.95

After the publication of her hugely successful first book Alice was inundated with fan mail urging her to put pen to paper once more. The result is this, her second volume of memoirs in which she shares with us yet another exciting and eventful year in her life.

*Alice's Adventures* is full of the wry, witty observations on life which so delighted the readers of her first book, and the wonderful illustrations capture the most poignant moments of the year.

**".. as far as Alice's Diary and Alice's Adventures are concerned nothing would persuade me to part with my copies of these two books for I have had hours of delight in reading them"**
(Miss W., Cheshire)

*Order from Publishing House, Trinity Place, Barnstaple, Devon EX32 9HJ, England*

# The Bilbury Chronicles £12.95 (hardback)

A young doctor arrives to begin work in the small village of Bilbury. This picturesque hamlet is home to some memorable characters who have many a tale to tell, and Vernon Coleman weaves together a superb story full of humour and anecdotes. The Bilbury books will transport you back to the days of old-fashioned, traditional village life where you never needed to lock your door, and when a helping hand was only ever a moment away. The first novel in the series.

"I am just putting pen to paper to say how very much I enjoyed The Bilbury Chronicles. I just can't wait to read the others."
(Mrs K., Cambs)

"...a real delight from cover to cover. As the first in a series it holds out the promise of entertaining things to come"
(Daily Examiner)

"The Bilbury novels are just what I've been looking for. They are a pleasure to read over and over again"
(Mrs C., Lancs)

# Bilbury Grange £12.95 (hardback)

The second novel in the Bilbury series sees the now married doctor moving into his new home - a vast and rambling country house in desperate need of renovation. With repair bills soaring and money scarce, the doctor and his new wife look for additional ways to make ends meet. Another super novel in this series - perfect for hours of escapism!

"I have just finished reading Bilbury Grange. I found the book to be brilliant. I felt as though I was part of the community. Please keep me informed of any more in this excellent series."
(Mr C, Cleethorpes)

"A wonderful book for relaxing and unwinding. Makes you want to up roots and move to the rural heartland."
(Lincolnshire Echo)

"For sheer relaxing pleasure here's another witty tale from the doctor whose prolific writings are so well known."
(Bookshelf)

*Order from Publishing House, Trinity Place, Barnstaple, Devon EX32 9HJ, England*

## The Bilbury Revels £12.95 (hardback)

Disaster strikes in this the third Bilbury novel when a vicious storm descends on the village. The ensuing snow storm cuts off the village and blankets the whole area in a deep carpet of snow. Much damage is done to the village as a result of the storm and the locals band together to undertake the repair work. Money, as ever, is tight and fund-raising is of prime importance. Money-spinning suggestions are sought and so the idea of the Revels is born - a week of fun and festivities to raise the money needed to repair the local schoolteacher's cottage.

## Bilbury Country £12.95 (hardback)

Well over half a million readers have already discovered the joy of life in North Devon through Vernon Coleman's previous Bilbury books. The colourful characters who inhabit this fictional Exmoor village have yet another battle on their hands in this fourth novel when a newspaper article turns a trickle of tourists into a veritable flood! The villagers have a dilemma on their hands - do they give thanks for the much-needed financial boost from the hoard of visitors; or do they try to stem the tide of tourists in an attempt to regain the peace and tranquillity they love so much

## Bilbury Pie £12.95 (hardback)

A delightful collection of short stories based in and around this fictional Devon village.

Every community has its characters and Bilbury is no exception! Thumper Robinson is the local "jack the lad" and Pete is the taxi driver, shop owner, funeral director and postman all rolled into one. Patchy Fogg dispenses advice on antiques to anyone who will listen and Dr Brownlow is the eccentric and rather elderly, retired local doctor

*Order from Publishing House, Trinity Place, Barnstaple, Devon EX32 9HJ, England*

## Mrs Caldicot's Cabbage War £12.95 (hardback)

A truly inspiring novel about a woman who embarks on the adventure of a lifetime following the unexpected death of her husband. Pushed from pillar to post by an uncaring family who are determined to rule her life, she fights back with amazing results. Full of the gentle humour and wonderful storytelling for which Vernon Coleman is so well-loved.

**"Thank you so much for Mrs Caldicot's Cabbage War. All your books are great."**
(Mrs N., Surrey)

**"Vernon Coleman writes stories liberally sprinkled with gentle humour, colourful characters and anecdotes"**
(Bolton Evening News )

**" ... quite hilarious and my sort of reading"**
(Mrs C., Darwen )

**"A splendid relaxing read"**
(Sunday Independent)

## Deadline £12.95 (hardback)

After losing his job on a national newspaper, Mark Watson is approached by a former colleague whose wife has mysteriously disappeared. Despite his total lack of experience, Watson finds himself offering to help locate the missing woman. Before he know it has finds himself embarked on a new career - that of private investigator. You'll be gripped by this thriller set in London and Paris.

**"We enjoyed Deadline - it was worth waiting for"**
(E.B., Chatham )

**"An excellent book"**
(D.D.S. London )

*Order from Publishing House, Trinity Place, Barnstaple, Devon*
*EX32 9HJ, England*